On The Edge of Red

How I Achieved a Modicum of Success and Remained Sane in Nearly 40 years of High School Teaching

by
Kurt L. Kromholtz

authorHOUSE™

1663 LIBERTY DRIVE, SUITE 200
BLOOMINGTON, INDIANA 47403
(800) 839-8640
WWW.AUTHORHOUSE.COM

First published by AuthorHouse 12/02/05

ISBN: 1-4208-9506-0 (sc)

Printed in the United States of America
Bloomington, Indiana

This book is printed on acid-free paper.

Kurt L. Kromholtz

B.S. Chemistry, Gonzaga University, 1959

Secondary Level Teaching Credentials,
University of Washington, 1964

M.S. Chemistry, Purdue University, 1970

Electronic Technician's Credentials,
DeVry Institute, 1975

This book is dedicated to my wonderful mother, God rest her soul, without whose unflinching tutelage and encouragement my successes would never have happened.

Dedicated to
Winifred Marjorie (Stevens) Kromholtz,
1907 -2000

- - - Kurt Kromholtz , October, 2005

Acknowledgements

Bryan Kromholtz, O.P. the youngest of my
three sons, a Dominican, Catholic priest now studying
in Switzerland, who generously dedicated many hours
of his considerable talents to various vital aspects of this
project, including multiple proof readings and publication
suggestions.

Sharon (Crawford) Kromholtz. My lovely wife of
forty-six years,herself a college English major,who not only
contributed much in proof reading and sentence structure
advising, but actually came up with the book title and
whose gentle prodding got me started in the first place.

Table of Contents

Preface

I had always wanted to teach, but for many years out of college, I was afraid to venture there because of two warnings I had heard: (1) it didn't pay adequately, and (2) student lack of discipline made the job too unpleasant and stressful. However, I was forced to make the fateful decision when a huge layoff by the Aerospace company that I worked for finally added me, then a young "materials engineer" with no seniority, to the layoff list. I don't regret the career move because of the tremendous satisfaction teaching has brought me.

After my retirement from teaching in 2002, with around 40 total years of experience working with teenagers at the high school level, my wife and family have convinced me to share my learning experiences with others. The following, then, is just that: some of the classroom vignettes that illustrate many of those lessons in the real art of teaching which cannot be learned in college classes in "education" theory, but are driven home in the actual angst of classroom give and take. I have also included a little autobiographical information to help explain my motivation and leanings. I hope some readers may find this stuff useful, and, maybe, mildly entertaining!

The rather unusual title of this book bears some explanation. The idea for the title "popped up" one winter day when my wife and I were checking out the operating temperature of the little pellet stove we use to augment our main heating system at our 90 year old, 2-story frame home. The little circular-shaped, magnetic dial-type thermometer is firmly attached to a heated wall of the stove and its pointer continuously monitors stove temperature with enough accuracy to allow us to maintain good heat production without danger of overheating. The dial is calibrated to show a danger, or "red zone," above which the manufacturer of the stove warns not to stray for long. My wife suddenly exclaimed "Kurt! There, finally, is a catchy title for your book!" And the rest is history.

Over the many years I spent in the high school classroom, both as a student, teacher, and as a formal observer, and also from watching dozens of my colleagues and their teaching approaches, I have become convinced that the single most important rule for the classroom teacher never to forget is to keep one's temper and composure at all costs, that is to remain only on the edge of red. I have seen some situations where an initial refusal to act on what seemed at the time to be a rather harmless, student infraction, appeared to be the easier route; however, this often led to an escalation of bad behavior, and eventually the beleaguered teacher would "blow his stack" over some relatively minor thing, and in some cases would cause irretrievable, regretted insults or even physical harm to the student who had finally, gleefully, pushed the teacher over the edge and into the "red zone," where mindless rage takes over reason.

One fellow teacher comes to mind, who would never even verbally reprimand his students, no matter how obnoxious they were. Finally he blew up and "decked" a boy in his class over a small infraction. This teacher was summarily fired, whereupon he was later sanctioned for the very same act in a different school district.

High school students instantly lose respect for any teacher who cannot control anger, and administrations and school boards, in my experience, invariably are forced to come down hard on a teacher who has "lost it" and acted on an impulse of rage. Actually, you don't do yourself any favor, either, when you allow student behavior to escalate by failing to mete out mild punishment for small infractions, early on. Much of what follows in this book involves discussion of applications of this art of always calmly and purposefully remaining "on the EDGE of red." It takes some self-discipline, but it's not a bad place to be! Your health will be the better for it, as well.

There is another side to this coin which is equally important. Teaching is really just another form of salesmanship. Every time you appear in front of your class you are selling your "product," namely your subject, to your students. Enthusiasm, therefore, is essential to your success. Thus, it is critical to maintain your optimistic, encouraging "edge," not only occasionally, but each and every day! You are always "on stage," so to speak, and so your attitudes are under continuous scrutiny, at least as much as your knowledge of your subject. I found that I practically never had a satisfying day of teaching if I had been feeling a little below par that day, for whatever reason. High school students, rightly or wrongly, expect their teachers to be almost superhumanly excited about their subjects. This is very hard on some people, I realize, but this trait was never a problem for this writer, since I was always in love with the subjects I taught! This gave me a big advantage from the start, and I have to say here at the outset, I would not recommend the teaching vocation to anyone who wasn't already thoroughly convinced that his or her subject was the greatest academic pursuit out there! The competition for the kids' minds in high school is fierce, and only the most aggressive, enthusiastic mentors will win over the interest of the students. Some jobs don't work that way, necessarily. In fact, back in the days I was doing materials research and development, I found my naturally ebullient, enthusiastic personality a bit of a detriment, from time to time, because what was most often needed for that kind of endeavor was a more steady, almost plodding approach, which, unlike my excitement-craving nature, would lend itself to an appropriate, long-term precision and attention to detail, much of which brought to me an eventually unacceptable level of frustration and boredom. I simply began to feel "out of it." Thus, the teacher must maintain his or her "edge" of expectations, if the truly effective, dynamic relationship needed there is to be established, and if the desired results are ultimately to be achieved. Once again, you always need to be "on the edge of red."

Phlegmatic types, reconsider this career area, I beg you: it will not likely be your cup of tea!

Note: In actual classroom exchange situations presented, I have used boldface type for my own dialogue. (That's me talking.) Also, I have changed some of the names to maintain the anonymity of those involved.

Chapter 1

Chemistry Beckons

I was always a pretty good student in grade (elementary) school, and most of the credit for that has to go to my mother. She was a partially college-educated, would-be "schoolmarm" of British-Canadian ancestry, and she always wanted me and my four siblings to "make something of ourselves" in life. My family was far from well-off, but my courageous mother, by an almost miraculous juggling of their meager funds, always saw to it that we kids remained enrolled in good quality parochial (Catholic) schools. In addition to this she continuously monitored the academic progress of all of her five, boisterous children, and by patient, daily tutoring helped turn us all into self-confident writers! My good-hearted, but uneducated (and totally intellectually outclassed) father managed to keep our bodies and souls together by working a series of unskilled labor type jobs, and remained tolerant of my mother's "big ideas" (as he referred to them) for our futures in education. To be fair to my father, it must be pointed out that he had "bailed out" of high school after only one year, in large part because most of his friends, and neighbors had done the same in order to take immediate, relatively high-paying union jobs in the local, big, profitable sawmill in their small Montana town. In those days college was thought to be for "rich folks" only, and the sawmill jobs, as they were for hundreds of his peers, could have been adequate, but an industrial accident had caused my father to lose the sight in one eye, and rendered him ineligible for his former job status. Thus, my parents had been forced, shortly after the mishap, to move to the "big city" to find unskilled employment for my father. My dad, although uneducated, and a bit resentful for the loss of a decent weekly paycheck, steadfastly worked a string of low-level, occasionally somewhat dangerous jobs to pay our bills throughout the 1940's and 50's. My father was, in many ways, a very fine person, and was held in much esteem by his own family. I'll never forget one of his brothers (my uncle) telling me, out of my father's earshot,

"You know, Kurt, Louis (my dad) always managed to find a job, even during the depression, when the rest of us couldn't find a thing, he would beat the bushes until he had one!"

The guy was conscientious to a fault, honest, faithful to our family and to his Catholic faith, and very hard-working. I am proud to think he may have passed on some of those qualities to me. He found the prospect of college for me scary indeed, and although I didn't understand his reluctance at the time, it is obvious to me now.

In addition to our lack of income, my mother was a totally convinced, whole-hearted convert to Catholicism, with its then-insistence on the terrible evils of "artificial" contraception, meaning a continuous string of pregnancies for her, and she felt her duty was to be a "stay-at-home" mommy to me (I am the oldest) and my rapidly growing contingent of siblings. I think that for a guy who got married so late in life, who had been 35 years old, a Marine and Merchant-Marine veteran, and who had had no dependents for all those single, post-high school years, the responsibilities that rushed in upon my father, right after his marriage to my mother in 1936, must have just appalled him! However, it was my relatively unsophisticated father, not my well-bred, education-conscious mother who unwittingly gave me my start in chemistry as a career.

I remember vividly during the Christmas season of 1946, the big day was only a week or two off, and, as my mother told me later, they had, as yet, still not decided on what would be my gift. Anyway, my father said to me, one Saturday, "Son, would you like to take a little trip downtown to see some of the department store toy departments?" I was so surprised at the offer and thrilled at the prospect, I replied,

"Wow, sure, let's go!"

We saw a number of interesting offerings, but when we finally came to a display of "Gilbert Chemistry Outfits" I remember well,exclaiming

"Boy, I sure would like to have one of these!"

What happened next still astounds me to this very day. My dad's eyes lit up and he said to me

"Kurt, I'm getting hungry. I'll bet you are,too. Why don't we go down a floor to the soda fountain and get a little lunch?"

I agreed and reluctantly left the magical display and went on down to the little lunch bar with him, and was soon chomping on a Coney Island style hot dog accompanied by a big glass of the store's own special root beer soda pop.

Dad immediately said to me,

"Son, I left something upstairs in the toy department. I'll be right back. Go ahead and finish your lunch," whereupon he walked briskly away to the stairs at the far east end of the store. I do not know what possessed me, but with absolutely no hesitation or planning at all, I promptly and without his seeing me, *followed* him as he made his way back to that chemistry set display, and I, guiltily and delightedly, watched him purchase that chemistry set for me! I, then with great haste, sneaked back to the lunch bar where I gobbled what was left of my lunch, all the while feeling guilty as could be (I still do!) but thrilled at the prospect of ownership of the kit, sure to be mine in a week or two. From then on, until that fateful Christmas I feigned ignorance of my expected gift, and on Christmas morning I am sure I must have exhibited way too much surprise when I opened that package. But, to be sure, I fell head over heels in love with that little kit, and proceeded to carry out every experiment in that beginner's manual. In fact, I liked it so much, I soon ran out of the tiny supply of chemicals that were included with the set, so my mother, thrilled to see me finally interested in something more than "Superman" or "Captain Marvel" comic books, ferreted out a local retail chemical supply outlet, and began to see that my little wooden containers were replenished. I got so mesmerized, I soon was trading my remaining meager supply of personal possessions for chemistry sets which other kids had owned and quickly lost interest in. Before long I saw "Porter Chemcraft" and "Lionel Chem-Lab" sets added to my little bedroom layout, to name a few, and soon was haunting the libraries for more books on "home chemistry" experiments. Birthdays and such added more apparatus and glassware, and next I was forced to move everything to our basement because of the nasty smells the experiments were producing. There my laboratory really blossomed, finally taking up a whole west wall right next to my father's tool bench. And I was barely nine years old! I began to develop a neighborhood reputation as some sort of "mad scientist" because of the small explosions I regularly showed off to neighborhood kids, and, I found out, much later, their parents were all most curious as to what exactly went on behind that lit-up basement window on the west side of my folks' home on those cold winter nights. Actually, mostly, it was pretty innocuous, since I had gotten interested in running little chemical "magic shows" and charged a tiny admission to those buddies interested enough to appear at my basement door.

"Okay, now I'll change water to wine and wine to milk" and I proceeded to dump out the foul, white suspension before some skeptical kid could demand "drink it, drink it!"

I never reflected on it at the time , but it was right there that I got the very first "kick" out of showing others something "cool" in chemistry, and actually enjoyed doing that even more than the experiment itself. The teacher in me was already emerging, and I had not recognized it, at all.

As I grew older, and with the advent of Sputnik, followed by the American space program in the late '50s I began to become interested in rockets and, together with some of my more scholarly young buddies, started to build small model rockets in that basement lab. One incident comes immediately to mind. Together with a friend, John, I had fashioned a little solid-propelled model rocket, complete with wings and tail. One day we had placed the little gadget on a "launching pad" (actually just a four-foot length of aluminum door molding) and had lit the end of the fuse, and pointed the "ramp" out toward the river that flowed through the city. For a couple of minutes the fuse burned away, shooting flames out of the rear of the aluminum tube fuselage, looking very, very impressive, but going nowhere since nothing could really happen until that fuse flame contacted the propellant in the main body of the rocket. Soon the flame subsided, and after another minute or so, appeared to have gone out. John then yelled,

"I think it went out. I'm gonna go take a look!"

I shot back, urgently,

"No, no, John, don't go near it!"

But to no avail. John not only went right over to the smoldering contraption, **but squatted down and peered right up into its rear end!** Just at that exact moment the fuse flame came into contact with the main body of propellant, and WHAMMO! That little aluminum tube rocket shot out of there like a bullet from a gun, spewing out a big flame and lots of blue smoke. I ran from behind a little tree I had been using for a shield to John's side, fearing the worst. John's face was totally blackened by the smoke but he had instinctively and instantly closed his eyes and had sprung back away from the gadget, avoiding any serious damage. Meanwhile the rocket was **tumbling** out over the river, and looking down at the pad, we could see why: the fuselage had left its wings and tail there, still in their original locations relative to the rocket body! The hysterical laugh which we both uttered, I think, did much to neutralize the severe scare we'd just had. We had the chemistry right, but what we **didn't** know about metal work would have filled many volumes. We had tried to **solder** the steel wings and tail to the aluminum fuselage! My friends and I never did have any big-time success with model rocketry, mostly due to our own impatience, and lack of in-depth technical know-how, but we certainly had a lot of fun, and you can see that my future as a chemist, a rocket scientist, and ultimately, a teacher, clearly was sealed when I was a young child.

My first experience with an official academic course in chemistry came when I enrolled in Mr. Burns' high-powered (honors) beginning general chemistry course, ironically at the very same high school at which I was destined to teach, many years later. Mr. Burns was a tall, lean, intense (and brilliant) Jesuit scholastic (not yet ordained priest) who wanted our class to do very well in the end-of-the-year "province" exams, and so poured it to us, really putting my "feet to the fire" that year. He was tough, but fair, and I got a good preparation there for the onslaught I would later encounter as a chemistry major at Gonzaga University. I'll never forget him for one distinct classroom memory. One day, after posing at least ten or more questions to the class, out of frustration at being unable to stump me on any of them, he suddenly stood up and hurled a copy of **Weast's CRC Handbook of Physics and Chemistry (36th Edition)** at me, yelling

"Here, Kromholtz, you might as well have this. You already know it all, anyway!"

I'll never forget reaching up to catch that flying missile, its thousands of little tissue-paper thin pages wildly flapping in the air. I kept that thick, little manual all through college, graduate school and beyond as my most-used reference source. Because of my great interest in the subject I stayed tops in that chemistry class all year, and from that day on I began to get a reputation as some sort of science nut. My classmates started calling me "the electron," which moniker, thankfully, didn't stick past high school. But, at that point, after high school graduation, I decided to pursue seriously a college degree in chemistry, which I did, to my mother's delight, and my poor father's initial chagrin. I enrolled as a chemistry major at Gonzaga University in the fall of 1955, and found that this was certainly no longer high school! I had a tough first semester, but soon learned good study habits, and finally settled in for a successful four-year effort, culminating in a B.S. in chemistry in 1959. Fortunately I turned out to be pretty adept at obtaining summer employment. I worked quite a spectrum of summer jobs over that four years, including grocery delivery, contract house painting, and then obtained employment with the Great Northern Railway Co., first as a "Gandy Dancer"(section gang hand), then as a switchman, and finally, set poles at 6000 ft. altitudes in the Montana Rocky mountains with the railroad's telegraph crew (hardest physical labor I've ever done!). I managed to save nearly every penny I made those summers, often mailing my paychecks home on payday, before I could lose the money in some stupid poker game, which most of the hands expected us "college punks" to join on Friday evenings (payday). Many of those non-college guys would be suckered in and lose their whole paycheck they had just spent a tough week earning. I can remember how glad I was, when those cowboys and Indians (they really were!) would try to coax me into a game, to be able to say without lying, **"Hey, you can have any money you can find on me!"**

I was able in this way to pay nearly all of my college expenses for the full four years, which was a tremendous boon to my beleaguered father, I am sure.

I was enjoying my chemistry training thoroughly, until an incident in general chemistry lab, one day, my freshman year, taught me and my fellow chem majors a little bit about the dangers of that subject. On the west wall of the lab was kept a cache of 3 or 4 very large bottles (4-5 gallon size, each) of the strong, mineral acids, the color-coded caps of which had become sloppy-fitting with age and crystallization. On this particular day, with time running short in the session, one very handsome classmate of mine, Roy, in a hurry to finish his experimentation, scurried to the acid nook, grabbed a carboy of nitric acid and leaped back to his lab station, planning to quickly replenish his supply of the foul-smelling, fuming liquid. But he had **grasped the bottle by its lid,** and the loose fit caused the bottle to drop out of its cap and hit the floor with a loud "thud." When the bottle hit the floor, a large "swoosh" of the nasty stuff shot out of the bottle's neck like a fire hose blasting right into Roy's face! Being closest to him, I had witnessed the whole thing, and I yelled to my lab partner

"Dick, help me with this, now!"

At that, Dick (later a Ph.D. in chemical engineering) and I together dragged Roy over to the nearest sink, forced his head under the faucet and ran water over his face for about five minutes. Fortunately for Roy, he had instantly closed his eyes, so they were unharmed, but his facial skin had been badly burned and the boy was out of school for a few days. When he returned his face was covered with a grotesque brown scab, making him almost impossible to look at. We were all shocked, wondering if he was permanently disfigured. (After a couple of weeks, though, the scab began to peel off slowly, revealing the most perfect skin beneath that any of us had ever seen. When all of the scab had been removed, Roy had lost his eyebrows, eyelashes, every mole, wart, freckle or pimple, plus a good frontal patch of his hair, but his complexion was as fresh as a baby's! Soon he was totally recovered, even handsomer than before. I don't recommend this approach for dermatological therapy, but I understand the "nitric acid dam" approach has been effective for some severe cases of acne, when properly executed by a trained physician.) In any case, we learned that chemistry could bite you! I, unlike many of the other students, had already been well aware of the dangers, because of my experiments with model rocketry, but this mishap had been a real wake-up call to all of us. I continued to love the subject, but we all were learning to respect it, as well. Experiences such as this, I can see, served to introduce a healthy wariness into my teaching approach which contributed to my successes in conducting future high school lab sessions.

Chapter 2

High School is "Where It's At"

I was no stranger to teaching. As a senior (4th year) chemistry major at Gonzaga University in Spokane, Washington, I decided to sign up as a "lab assistant" to the very fine general chemistry professor there (a Jesuit priest with his Ph. D from Catholic University, Washington, D.C.), a published perfume chemist with patents of his own, whose class was especially designed for freshman chemistry and chemical engineering majors. I was excited to get the job because I needed the "pin money" and because this professor I would be working under was a wonderful teacher and a fine human being: a real professional and a true gentleman whom we students who had taken his class as freshmen had respected mightily (and still did) for his infectious enthusiasm both for the subject and for life.

As lab assistant, I was expected to make sure that students were prepared for that afternoon's exercise. In addition, one of my duties was to answer the students' questions both on the lab exercise itself and on the theory behind it. I found being "on stage" this way stimulating and goal-directing, since it made my knowledge come alive; and, provided I was well-prepared, I felt that I was, in a small way, helping young people of the same aspirations as my own to realize more success in their career training. I also found, during that time as a teaching assistant (or "T.A." as we were called), that the old adage is true, that "you never learn anything as well, as when you have to teach it." I think it was there that I first got that "kick" from helping others succeed that would some day become my prime motivator. However, discipline was not an issue in this setting, as these were all young men and women who were totally motivated, and hoped to graduate as chemists or chemical engineers in about four years. Because of the difficulty of the program, typically only about a quarter of the original group would actually make it to graduation as a chemist or chemical engineer. Case in point: I was, fortunately, one of only seven of the original twenty-four who had started in my freshman-year class who actually graduated four years later with the desired B.S. degree in chemistry.I actually graduated with a double major, chemistry and mathematics. I had also been lucky to get authorization to do my "undergraduate thesis"(then required for American Chemical Society accreditation) on a pet topic of mine, namely "Mathematical Aspects of Solid Rocket Propellant Chemistry "

I'm sure that was a factor in my obtaining the wonderful job I got with LLNL right after graduation.

About that same time, when I was a freshman in college, the Korean conflict had started, so I joined the Washington Army National Guard in an infantry company. I worked my way up through the ranks from buck private to Sergeant First Class, largely on my then-improving ability to "give classes." I taught close-order drill, manual-of-arms, and fire-and-maneuver techniques, to mention a few topics, and developed a "no-nonsense" demeanor which earned the respect of my fellow soldiers and some accolades from my commanding officers. In fact, at one summer camp at Fort Lewis, Washington, I was designated "non-com of the day" for that particular regiment because the officer who happened to drop by on his rounds to inspect various classes in the field was favorably impressed with my class and recommended me for Officer's Candidate School as well as the award. I soon became a major instructor for that unit(my company) at the weekly evening drill sessions, and later specialized in group marching exercises. At one of my annual two-week summer camp training sessions I managed to qualify as our company's representative in the annual regimental manual-of-arms "drill-down" contest, coming in an exhausted second place out of hundreds of participants. I was kinda "gung-ho," I guess, for a while there, and I have to say, after being promoted to drill sergeant,("E-6") it was heady stuff to direct the movement of 30 to 40 men, many of whom were not exactly docile types, if you know what I mean. I think it was there that I developed a measure of self-confidence, every bit of which, little did I know, I would later need for my high school teaching days.

For a short while there, I was understandably torn between continuing with chemistry as my career goal or pursuing the military (officer's candidate school) until the choice was made easier by a bizarre incident. At that time I was not only a member of the Washington Army National Guard, but by virtue of a government contract that Gonzaga University had signed, was required to participate in "Military Science" classes and training at the college. This was actually Army R.O.T.C., and all healthy, male students were required to take part, if the draft were to be avoided. Each spring my National Guard outfit had been pleased to march, in full dress uniform, with contingents from all the other local military service reserve units, in the annual "Lilac Festival Armed Forces Day" parade. I had always enjoyed this function, since I had been a drill sergeant myself, and had taught and competed in close-order drill, as I mentioned above. This year, however, things were different. I got orders, not only from the Guard commanding officer, but also from the R.O.T.C. commander, to report, the next Saturday morning, for staging followed by marching with both units!. Not having yet mastered **bilocation**, I immediately obtained a meeting with the R.O.T.C commander, telling him of my predicament. He loudly proclaimed

"Soldier, you will march with **this** unit, is that understood?"

I saluted and left, but I didn't understand. Next, I obtained an "audience" with my National Guard company commander, a highly

15

respected former regular Army captain, who had been, it was said, a decorated member of the elite Army **Rangers** unit in World War II. I saluted and told him about my problem concerning my orders from the R.O.T.C commander, to march with that unit, or else. He leaned back in his desk chair, looked hard at me and calmly said,

"Sergeant Kromholtz, you **will** march with the National Guard, as usual, on Saturday. That's an order."

At that moment I realized that my only hope was my own creativity, so I asked myself one question: "What will happen to me if I don't march with the R.O.T.C?" The answer, I realized, was that I would get a few demerits which would likely lower my semester grade a little in that low credit-hour course in military science. When I applied the same question to the National Guard, I knew, as was his custom, the company commander would likely send out the M.P.'s to pick me up, and I could even be demoted, and/or court-martialed So, come Saturday, there I was again, in the full dress regalia of "Baker company, 1st battalion, 161st Infantry Regiment, Washington National Guard," and vowing with renewed vigor to continue my pursuit of chemistry, not the military, as a career!

Fortunately for my career aspirations, it was at just about that time that the Korean armistice was signed, so the conscription pressure lightened up considerably, allowing me some career related opportunities, and, upon graduation from "G.U." I landed a superb job in my own special area, namely rocket research, at the Lawrence Livermore National Laboratory (LLNL, then called UCRL, the

University of California Radiation Laboratory) promptly married my sweetheart of three years, and began what would be my early non-teaching "pre-career" in that little post-war boomtown of Livermore, California. After just a couple of years there, absorbing as much of the state of the art as I could, a physicist friend of mine invited me to apply for a job with a big company in the Pacific Northwest, which I did, was hired, and then proceeded to uproot my now growing family to move north. I had been wanting to move my family to the Pacific Northwest for some time and this was my opportunity, I thought.

A few years later, when I and a thousand other "engineers" (as we were called) were laid off by the aerospace company I had been working for, I decided to go after my teaching credentials, which I obtained in roughly a year's work at the University of Washington, in Seattle. Next, I quickly found a temporary job teaching mathematics at a local community college. These were all young men and women, who, for various reasons had not gotten into a four year university, and were hoping to make out okay in my class so as to be finally accepted into the university of their choice. They were scared to death, and I was absolutely unable to relax them enough so they could even laugh at one of my silly jokes. I believe it was that one semester of nervous academic struggle which convinced me I was not cut out to be a college instructor. These kids were just **too** serious! I think it was just about then that I began to realize that maybe, just maybe, high school might be my calling. After all, I had gotten my teaching credentials doing my student teaching (then called "cadet teaching") at one of the local high schools and had gotten considerable accolades from my supervising teacher, along with the big hunk of college credit which always went with a good grade in that aspect of college training in educational techniques. I remember various friends and relatives expressing disbelief when they heard of my plans to try secondary level education. I remember one of my aunts exclaiming something like,

"Good heavens, Kurt, we remember how you used to say when you were in high school that you couldn't imagine doing that for a living, what with the stress your own high school teachers were going through. You wanted to make more money, work in a high-tech laboratory, and have the status that an industrial chemist or engineer would have, not to contend with a bunch of unruly kids (like I was) who some times didn't really want to be there and who went out of their way regularly to make life miserable for a given teacher."

Little did I know then that one day I'd be on the other end of that teacher/student discourse, and would learn to love it!

Down inside I never forgot the thrill I'd experienced in my own high school years of encountering a really competent classroom teacher. I was very fortunate to have had a few great ones, and we all just loved those guys and gals. They made you want to learn and made education look like the answer to all the world's problems. And for this writer, the very best I ever had were in high school. I still remember them vividly, and although I didn't know it at the time, they were eventually to be my most important role models. My life was most significantly shaped during those hormone-raging high school years, even though I probably would have denied it emphatically at the time. High school students are still easily inspired, still have their sense of humor and rarely have developed a durable cynicism to stifle any thrill of learning. High school is "where it's at"! It's the most exciting place on the planet, once you figure out how it works.

Chapter 3

Success Brings Survival

"Mr. Braxton! Yes you, Mr. Braxton! Look at me, not at Mr. Mortenson. I'm the act here, not your classmate there, no matter how attractive he may be [class tittering]. Zip the lip. You know the rules. They haven't changed. If you have a question, raise your hand to be recognized, as always. Then I, your teacher, will try to answer your question for you. If you have a question on this concept, then I am sure others will, too."

[Boy scrunches down in his seat with guilty look on his face and asks no question. Rest of class is dead silent all during this exchange, each individual wondering what the fate of "Mr. Braxton" will be.]

I can clearly remember dozens of similar episodes in my career as a high school chemistry teacher; and the confidence needed to make such a desirable outcome occur, I can assure you, did not come overnight. My first year was an unmitigated disaster. I wanted so desperately to be liked and to be successful that I came on way too friendly, way too nice. My students saw this as weakness and proceeded to dismantle my program. Once credibility is lost, it is very difficult to recoup it. I never did achieve a healthy relationship with that first group. Somehow I limped through the remainder of that year, vowing to start right the next year. I was a nervous wreck that inaugural year, and many times wondered if I should return to my previous life as an aerospace rocket-scientist/engineer. At least the Saturn-5 rocket didn't talk back to me when I told it what to do!

The high school student is not purposefully cruel, but expects his or her teacher to be in charge and to have something worthwhile to accomplish. I'll never forget my first day at that originally all-boys high school. As I sauntered down the senior hall full of students rifling their lockers between classes, I overheard a boy say to his friend,

"Oh, Mr. Waltner, he makes us read 30 pages every night."

I remember thinking to myself at the time,

"How immature is that student, to act as though his teacher makes him do this or that"

Clearly, I had much to learn about the typical American teenager. That naiveté would nearly be my undoing, as it turned out.

21

I soon found out that, with very few exceptions, there is no such thing as an unsuccessful, long-lasting survivor in high-school teaching. You must do well just to maintain your sanity. The high school classroom is no place to hide, unlike many college classrooms, where lots of people of little teaching competence can find safe refuge from the demands of a real job. This is not to say that there are not many fine, capable teachers in the colleges and universities. Clearly, that is not the case. I have had many myself. Unfortunately, ownership of an advanced degree, a requirement for teaching at the college level, is no guarantee of teaching ability. In fact, many professors with Ph.D.'s that I have experienced were too wrapped up in their subject matter to be concerned about improving their classroom delivery. Once I realized that I had much to learn about the art of teaching, I finally began to succeed, and that brought peace of mind and tremendous satisfaction. I actually began to look forward to the next class, and grew to like, even **need** that little shot of adrenaline that always accompanied the beginning of a class.

Chapter 4

ABC Means "Always Be Cool"

In the teaching of chemistry, **demonstrations** of chemical principles are needed, almost daily, to illustrate the topic being presented, and are very effective in generating excitement over the subject, if done right. I have always enjoyed explosions, when properly controlled, and so did my students, I found out.

On one particular day, I made a couple of procedural errors, and a small bottle of supposedly non-touch-sensitive explosive, which my older students had successfully prepared the day before, went off in my left hand with a loud report as I was holding it up for my class to see. I was in the process of saying,

"This explosive material will behave itself, if it is not allowed to be heated up, since it is not shock-sensitive."

When the bottle went off, it drove four or five pieces of jagged glass into my left palm causing intense pain. Blood started to drip from my hand almost instantly. What I did next still amazes me to this day. I calmly stated that I must have made an error somewhere, and hiding my bleeding hand, I edged my way a few feet to the demonstration desk sink, placed my left hand under the running water faucet, and washed off the chemicals and shard sticking in my hand. All the while continuing to lecture on the importance of following lab safety rules when dealing with potentially explosive substances! The class was just spellbound! From then on, I vowed always to present an unruffled demeanor to the students, no matter what happened, since I found that they were not afraid to follow my directions in subsequent lab projects. Panic is catching, and so is confidence, even if feigned. Stay only on the EDGE of "red"!

Another incident where this sort of projected self-assurance approach was useful, but for a completely different reason, comes to mind. During the late '60s and early '70s the country was buffeted by an often very destructive drug-promoting subculture which was, along with the poorly prosecuted Vietnam War, putting enormous pressure on our young people. The "heavy metal" or "acid" rock groups, along with irresponsible, high-profile adult "gurus," like Timothy Leary and others, had been pushing the "turn on, tune in, drop out" approach which, in effect, asked teenagers to reject all that which had been heretofore held sacred or noble, such as organized religion, patriotism, or even idealistic romance, and to find their "true" selves through LSD or mescaline-induced introspective exploration, a form of narcissistic self-absorption which scorned the ideas of true love, or any form of self-sacrifice. This terrible "fad" was obviously influencing our students no less than others, and we teachers felt it part of our mission to do verbal battle with these influences almost daily.

One day, as I was lecturing on some vital-to-chemistry theory, which the students were obviously having some difficulty understanding, suddenly one boy threw up his hand, and after being recognized, had the audacity to say,

"Mr. Kromholtz, why do we have to study **junk** like this? I would much rather study my own mind."

I immediately, instinctively replied, with some sarcasm (I mildly regretted later), **"But Chris, just think how fast you'd run out of subject matter!"** The boy smiled, and just **nodded**, as many in the class applauded.

I was not about to apologize for my subject to anyone, especially when I felt that a matter of principle was at stake. Keeping my temper made my position just that much more effective.

Chapter 5

Do You Really Like <u>Teaching</u>?

"Kurt, are you coming to the faculty workshop session this evening? Remember, Dr. Franklin Colby of Southern Washington University will present his teaching tips class entitled 'Just because the class is quiet, does that mean learning is taking place?'" (My teacher buddy, Kevin, poking his head in my classroom door after school, wanted to know.)

"I can't guarantee it, Kevin. I'm not really quite ready for tomorrow's lab sessions, and I've got to hold them as scheduled, to prepare the kids for the big section test coming up on Friday. I'll come as soon as I get my stuff under control. Tell the principal I'd like to be there, but right now I am just not ready for tomorrow's classes. Have fun, Kevin, and say 'hi' to the gang!"

Actually, I knew the turnout would be sufficient if I never got there at all, since every school has its contingent of "educators" (those among the faculty whose greatest joy is the unending discussion of the latest **theories** of teaching,(many of which have not had much actual success in the classroom) and this school was no exception. Most theories sound good on paper and many of them have been successfully used to garner their creators advanced degrees in education, even though they often fail miserably when really applied by some poor, easily bamboozled classroom teacher, desperately searching for a remedy in classroom management techniques which might save his or her rapidly sinking ship.

Personally, I have become very skeptical of **untested** theories in education, whether dealing with classroom management (most common losers), delivery techniques, or demonstrations to illustrate concepts from the subject matter itself. I just can't get excited about 'em. I would get really excited about a student who came up with a marvelous insight in my class, or another, whose mother told me at the PTA meeting that her daughter just can't believe how much she likes my chemistry class, and is now planning to major in the subject in college. Makes my day! If you would get your jollies thataway, you might just belong "in the trenches," a classroom teacher, like me. If **theories** are what turn you on, you may be a budding "educator." If so, get out of the classroom as soon as possible, before it is too late. All true teachers are educators, but not all educators are teachers. Teaching takes a special breed of cat, like me. I love it, and I miss it. If I could have afforded to do it, I would have started sooner, and kept at it longer. But that's a story in itself.

Chapter 6

Go That Extra Mile

"Mr. and Mrs. McAtee, if your daughter really wants to improve her grade, I will be more than happy to meet with her after classes, in my classroom, one-on-one, for a little extra help. Let's do this first, since I know exactly where her difficulties are, plus the tuition you are paying already covers the cost. If you hire a tutor, it will be expensive, and the tutor may not be able to pinpoint the snag as quickly. If we try this approach but you see no improvement, then we'll consider other avenues, okay?"

As it turned out, in this case, this strategy worked almost like magic. Sara came twice a week with questions concerning various problems in chemistry, and together we solved them, steadily increasing both her confidence and her enjoyment of the subject. In fact this girl actually went from a "D" in the first semester to an "A" in the second!

To be totally honest about this, I must admit that Sara's experience was the most spectacular case I can remember, although there were many similar, albeit not quite so dramatically successful ones, and I can still see in my mind's eye the shining faces of each of them when their test papers were returned with an "A" or even a "B" in one of Mr. Kromholtz's famous "tough" tests. This strategy soon became a staple with me since I found that parents were impressed to see a teacher willing to give a little of his or her own time to "coach" their son or daughter, and it therefore bought me a world of good will, both from parents and from administrators and counselors. Some avoid this problem by simply raising everyone's grades: the students who are having difficulties then receive higher grades along with everyone else. But this apparent "easy way out" lowers the standards of the course; and unfortunately, this is the stock "answer" followed by many in today's secondary academic institutions. However, when the teacher provides extra help to a faltering but sincere student, he or she can be brought up to the standard of the class. Admittedly, you'll have to give up a little after-school "shooting the breeze" with cronies in the faculty lounge, but the dividends are huge, and well worth the small sacrifice. One caution, though: always leave the door to your classroom wide open during these one-on-one sessions, for obvious reasons!

Chapter 7

Handle It Yourself

"**Mr. Miller, that snotty attitude means you will report to this room right after school this evening to help me get this lab cleaned up [class dead silent]. Be here immediately after 6th period, and be ready to do some janitorial work. This lab is getting filthy.**"

"But Mr. K, why not just give me one period of JUG?" said he. "That way you wouldn't need to hang around after school, too."

"**No, my friend. This way I can get my own lab looking nice, and you and I will have a chance to get to know each other a little better, as well,**" I countered.

(JUG is the acronym for "Justice Under God," a Jesuit invention, a type of after-school detention period that may include some menial labor assigned to those students unlucky enough to be sent there for disciplinary purposes.) JUG sounded pretty good at first, but it didn't take me long to find out that its effectiveness as a deterrent was only as good as the person or persons who supervised it. In fact, unless it was well organized and run, it could actually be counter-productive, since high school students are not stupid. Word gets around very fast if JUG this year is a paper-tiger only, and therefore an empty threat. Running my own "JUG" sessions demanded a little more of me at first, but paid off enormous dividends down the road, especially those years when someone "loosy-goosy" (cavalier) was running the JUG program. I also found that the administration really appreciated this extra effort, since none of them looked forward to detention supervision, either! Whenever possible, handle the small discipline chores yourself, and if you are on the ball and act quickly and fairly, kids will never graduate to **serious** breaches of rules and regulations at all. You will be doing them a tremendous favor!

Another example of the effectiveness of this approach I recall specifically applies here. At one period of time we (the faculty) were all experiencing an unacceptable increase in student tardiness. We all agreed that the problem was probably due to the too-relaxed attitude of our present dean of discipline (then called "vice principal for student life") to this behavior. For a time a group of us got together and tried very hard to convince this fellow that this trend was unacceptable, but he, together with the principal of the time, dismissed us as "curmudgeons" and simply ignored this frightfully disruptive infraction, making matters steadily worse. Finally, I personally had had enough, and once again took matters into my own hands. I decided that although I couldn't change the school, I could at least eliminate this problem in my own classes. I was able to do it by introducing a system of academic sanctions which worked something like this: I would allow a certain number of unexcused tardies each school quarter (three, if I remember correctly). After that, each successive tardy would cause the offending student to find his quarter grade dropped one notch (say, from an "A" to a "B," for example). Once I had obtained the principal's okay on this approach, I found the method worked like "gangbusters," and soon other teachers were creating similar systems, with successes commensurate with their diligence in applying said procedures! The administrators even began to promote such individual classroom policies because they found fewer kids were being given detention sentences, meaning less work for them! Once again, individual responsibility had done the trick. Such doings may seem obvious to you, the reader, but I assure you, this kind of approach was considered positively eye-opening to the liberal, "avant-garde" administrative cadre of that day. They, it seemed, had to learn even the most common-sense requirements by sad experience. As for myself, what I had done was simply to put in place what was necessary to make my program work. While that principal said I was "innovative," I felt I had just been desperate! Fortunately, the next principal and his team, upon taking over, immediately put in place a very effective, strict, school-wide attendance/tardiness policy which allowed us teachers the luxury of dropping these individual approaches, which, although they had worked well in a given classroom, tended to cause some students to brand a few teachers, like myself, as "bad-asses" (tough guys) and others as "nice guys," which was obviously a source of constant friction the faculty was better off without. Ah, school politics… always in play, and always an art! I must admit, I don't much miss that aspect of the high school teaching game.

Chapter 8

Hair!

Much of my early teaching experience took place in the '60's and '70's. You'll remember how obsessed with their hair that generation of teenagers had become. The object for both sexes was to grow as much of it as possible. The girls all wore it long and straight, and parted in the exact middle. The boys tried to do likewise, but always left theirs somewhat unkempt, in order to avoid a "femmy" look, as they called it, then. Their biggest problem would be when they had considerable natural curl in their hair. In that case, the boys would really exploit this, "bush up" the "coif" tremendously to produce what was called the "Afro" look., appearing much like a dandelion gone to seed. Many of my fellow teachers were really put off by all the hair on the boys, but I just felt it was a passing fad, simply a fashion that would not last, and indeed, this turned out to be the case. However, as a teacher of chemistry, all this "brush" did create a special concern. In chemistry lab work, the usual energy source is the venerable Bunsen burner, and large flames and hair do not mix! Therefore, I had always required both sexes to tie back any long locks, keeping the hair out of harm's way, during experiments. However, I had not done any more than warn the students about their Afro-do's, up to this particular point in time. Once during a lab session, one rather unpopular boy, Tony, having a super-sized Afro-cut, strayed too close to his partnership's Bunsen burner. From my vantage point high on my raised teaching platform, I spotted his hair flame up and begin to disappear. I immediately hollered,

"Tony, your hair!"

His lab partner instantly swatted Tony's head, extinguishing the flame with one or two "whacks"; but all his pent-up dislike for Tony finally finding a legitimate outlet, he continued swatting Tony, eventually unleashing a veritable windmill of hits, knocking poor Tony to the floor, then jumping on him to continue wailing on the boy (while the class looked on, approvingly). Tony was now writhing around, trying to escape a "cure" that was worse than the disease! I directed some other boys to drag Tony's assailant off him, reluctantly reprimanded the attacker, and then told the class that, from this day on, all people sporting Afro's would be required to cover them with a scarf in lab work. Tony's hair grew totally back in a few weeks, but his personality was permanently improved, to the liking of all! This turned out to be the one and only hair flare-up incident I was ever to encounter.

It seemed I had to learn nearly everything the hard way! Being on the edge of red could certainly keep a school day from becoming too dull!

Chapter 9

Look the Part

One Saturday morning I awoke realizing that I had not finished my lab preparations for the upcoming week's rather complex experiments, and thought to myself,

"I'd better buzz up to the school right away and take care of some of those chores before my wife wakes up with all of her usual plans for my day."

This operation was a rather common occurrence for me, since it was becoming more and more difficult for me to find any uninterrupted time for planning and preparation during school hours. So I put on my usual weekend "grubbies" (casual garb) and drove quickly to the back entrance of the school building. I entered the long lower hall and proceeded down it toward my lab-classroom, expecting the school to be essentially deserted, as it often was on a weekend morning. However, this particular morning was different. Squatting there, fishing around in his own locker, which was near the door to my classroom, was one of my own students, Jay. I said to him, with a hint of sarcasm

"Jay, don't you ever go home? You are probably here to pick up your chem text, which you forgot to take home Friday, right? You are such a hard-working student!"

When Jay saw me his eyes got big as saucers and his mouth fairly dropped to his chest as he stammered "M-M-Mr. K-K-Kromholtz?" We then chatted for a few minutes about Friday night's football game and other small-talk items, and he ran off with his needed supplies while I entered my lab-classroom to take care of my planned tasks. I was puzzled by this student's obviously extreme nervousness, since he had always seemed pretty comfortable around me during school hours. Come Monday, Jay was there in class, carrying out his work with a relaxed and confident air, but I noticed him eyeing me periodically for reassurance. Suddenly it dawned on me: on Saturday, I was "out of uniform"! I don't think he had ever seen me not wearing a sportcoat and tie, my "official" teaching attire. I thought to myself,

"I'll bet the students think I wear this 'get-up' all the time—maybe even to bed at night!"

We're talking the late '60s here with the sudden arrival of the "hippie" anti-hero culture and its subsequent acceptance by the American teenager, always the first to embrace the newest fads in dress.

I was one among a few others on our faculty who had rejected this "dress-down" concept, so I had become very careful always to "dress professionally" while on campus. Actually, I had noticed, almost immediately, when I first started teaching there, that those teachers who had tried to show their "solidarity" with their students by dressing in casual attire like jeans and sweatshirts, instead of winning the students' approval and esteem, had brought themselves only scorn. So I decided not to go that route, and I am sure it was the right decision, for what was my purpose here, anyway? Was it to become "buddies" with a new batch of kids every year, or was it to help these young people learn habits of thought and behavior that would help them to survive and succeed in later life? I decided that only the latter was really worth the effort. Beads and overalls might attract to you a few temporary "chums," but when the chips were down, even those "chums" went elsewhere for advice or counsel on career choices, or course planning or other matters they knew were important to their futures. That dress shirt might not be as comfortable as a knit polo, and that tie might start to bind a little at the end of the day, but you'll be more comfortable in other, more important ways; and, provided you are reasonably fair, firm, and consistent to boot, you will get a bigger measure of respect from the student body for looking the part. The "flower children" were fond of murmuring,

"It is not important what one looks like. It is what's inside that counts."

In the final analysis that motto is actually true. The problem is that other people cannot, and may never, see the beauty of your inner soul, but everyone sees immediately what you appear to be, and rightly or wrongly, judges you accordingly. Also, kids expect mommies to look like mommies, cops to look like cops, firemen to look like firemen, and **teachers to look like teachers.** The hippies were wrong on at least one major issue: everyone does need heroes, and teachers, whether they like it or not, are therefore expected to be good role models by all segments of the community. Look the part… you'll likely soon feel the part, as well! You'll find it easier to keep from falling off the **edge** and into the forbidden "red zone" of student disrespect.

Chapter 10

The Field Trip

High school kids, it is well known, are very adept at getting a teacher "sidetracked." I was well aware of this continuous quest, my students always looking for some way to divert my attention from the task at hand, thereby reducing, at least momentarily, their workload. However, one day, in the heat of the moment, I "lost my head" and found myself saying, after I had just concluded a lecture-discussion session on nuclear fission, something like,

"Gang, this kind of nuclear reaction is often exploited by electrical power plants, which, if they are so designed, will actually produce more fuel than they use. As a bonus, if they are properly designed, they are non-polluting, unlike fossil-fuel plants. You probably weren't aware of it, but we have such a plant just a few

miles south of here. Maybe we should take a trip down there and
see it up close and personal, one of these days!"

The resulting roar of approval told me I had better set this thing
up A.S.A.P. So I looked around and found that the Westinghouse
Company was operating those reactor-based plants at that time, and
when I contacted them, they were very happy to show a group of
interested high school students around. I next chose a date, got the go-
ahead from Westinghouse, chartered a bus, and signed up thirty or so
students on a first-come-first-served basis. The day we left the kids were
excited, enthusiastic in large measure over legally getting out of that
day's classes (especially mine, which had a reputation as a demanding
course). The mood was joyous and the kids were all looking forward to
viewing such a modern scientific marvel (remember, this was all before
the Russian "Chernobyl," or the American "Three Mile Island" nuclear
disasters, so there was no skepticism to spoil the anticipation.) The
drive of approximately three-hours was over before we knew it and we
were deposited at the front office of the government reservation, where
we were met by three public relations experts especially trained for
these tours. We were ushered into a big meeting hall, enthusiastically
welcomed, and then shown a superb movie exhibiting in detail the
complete operation of their breeder reactor powered plant, called the
Fast-Flux Test Facility ("FFTF") including cutaway views of the reactor
itself, with all parts called out and labeled. Next we were treated to a nice
lunch, and the kids were wildly ready to go out and see this marvelous
reactor "in person." We were then loaded on a couple of smaller shuttle

buses, specifically designed for the purpose and we took the 5 minute ride out to the "FFTF" plant. We saw the huge building from a couple of miles away, with big power lines coming from it, and were really getting "juiced" to see this thing, at that point. Reaching the plant we were taken off the shuttles and given a short introductory speech, then special badges were attached to each of us. It was explained, that these were radiation dosage monitors, which were required by government regulation, and that they would be removed after the tour to check accurately the amount of radiation we had taken. We were assured that no problems were anticipated, that this was merely routine. After all this build-up, we were getting hugely excited to actually see something, and the guides said, "well, here she is!" and rolled back two large sliding doors revealing the object of our trip. Yup, there it was, looking for all the world like one mammoth, single concrete cinder block! It was as though the kids were all individual balloons, which had just been punctured. Words cannot express how "underwhelmed" we all were. Many of the students began to fidget and to scout around the sides of this gigantic monolith, hoping to discover some interesting attachment. On the bus trip back the kids were mercifully uncritical, and I just kept repeating how unfortunate it was that we could not see more of the interior of the reactor for safety reasons.

Word must have gotten around that Mr. Kromholtz's field trips were less than memorable, because I noticed much less begging from that day forward. If it had not been for the wonderful movie we were shown, the whole trip would have been essentially a bust, academically.

I will not say that was my last field trip, but it certainly was my last pre-trip build-up speech. I learned from that frustrating experience: to never promise what you cannot deliver!

Chapter 11

Divide and Conquer

One ordinary day, I had been socializing in the faculty lounge during my "preparation period" when the bells sounded heralding the school's daily lunch period. Realizing I needed to use the restroom before eating, and noticing that the faculty facility was in use, I decided to drop down a level and use the student restroom before returning upstairs for a leisurely lunch with faculty cronies. In order to reach the student lavatory, it was necessary to go through the student lunchroom (called the "cafeteria") so I soon found myself there during "first lunch" period, and as usual the big room was crowded to the doors with hundreds of students, many calmly sitting at the long tables, stuffing their faces and noisily talking with their peers. At this particular school, teachers were asked to supervise daily, two at a time, on a rotating basis, and this was not a popular duty among the faculty, to say the least. On this occasion, the noise level, it seemed to me, was unusually high even for the notorious cafeteria, and I immediately saw why: a group of twenty or so students had left their seats and were milling around in the center of the room, yelling and jostling one another menacingly, while the two unfortunate teacher-supervisors on duty that day were cowering off to one side pretending not to notice what was obviously a brewing mob activity of some sort. I immediately went to the two "prefects" as they were called and voiced my concern, since I "smelled" an impending food-fight or some such. One teacher pooh-poohed my concern and walked away in a huff. The other, a huge guy with a booming voice, stepped up on a chair and shouted loudly enough to be heard by all: "All right, gang, everyone sit down, and pick up the trash you left on your tables. I'll be around with a garbage can in a minute!" The result was a resounding series of hoots and hollers of derision from the noisy twenty, and sarcastic laughter from what seemed to be the whole remaining student body. I could see the "supervisors" were rapidly losing control of the situation, even though one of them was physically very large. Rapidly scanning the twenty or so agitators, I spotted one whom I judged to be a ringleader. I then stared at him and him alone and waded right into the center of the group until I was standing nose to nose with just him. In a quiet voice I said to him,

"You stay around here when the lunch period is over. You and I need to have a little chat"

Meanwhile the cafeteria had gone dead silent, and some students were already starting to clean up their tables. Later I meted out some detention (JUG) punishment for the misbehavior exhibited by that one student and from that time on the cafeteria would calm down a little whenever I would enter it.

It was clear to me that high school students respond best when they are treated as individuals. In fact, this one-on-one approach was very effective in the classroom, as well, I soon found. They like their leaders calm, fair, firm, and consistent. Any breeches of those qualities will reduce the level of respect afforded a given faculty member. I was not a big man physically, and I have seen a petite, but seemingly fearless and resolute **woman** get the same level of respect, the same results, under similar circumstances. Teenagers, underneath that blustering, sometimes obnoxious facade they display to appear "cool" to their peers, actually want good, solid direction, especially from someone they admire. What's more, they desperately **want** to have someone to admire! Learn their names if possible, and get to know as many as you can as soon as you can. They'll love it. They'll love you, even if they have to work for you after school, or take a low grade when they didn't earn a higher one.

Chapter 12

The Invasion of the Coeds

I mentioned before that this was originally an all-boys school. After a few years (around ten to be more precise) the school was encountering financial difficulties, mainly because of a recent drop in religious vocations, requiring the employment of more and more lay instructors who, like myself, would not, or could not work for "peanuts" as the good fathers and sisters had done for so many decades. The two all-girls schools in the area were experiencing similar problems. At this particular moment, at the girls' school nearest us, they were finding it particularly difficult to find qualified science teachers, especially for physics and chemistry, whom they could afford to pay. Keep all this in mind as I continue. Soon, as was inevitable, the administrations of the schools began to meet to try to pool knowledge, and maybe come up with solutions to their common problems. Our principal, always wishing to cooperate with the diocese at large, began to attend these meetings regularly. Eventually one suggestion surfaced, as we knew it would, that a merger of our school with one or both of the girls schools might be the only answer. Our school had a younger, more well trained faculty, and had a decidedly larger building, but we were in need of more students, so the plan was to close the girls school nearest us and have the girls join our previously all-boy student body. When this idea was first mentioned to our faculty at a meeting, you'd have thought we were being asked to "walk the plank" or some such. There was absolutely no interest in the concept. How could the principal even consider bringing **girls** into our "hallowed halls"? The idea was temporarily shelved, since most of our teachers felt that the old, separated approach was not only a good one, but the **only** one! Hadn't we had great success, both academically, and athletically for decades? (This school **was** founded in 1889!) The principal finally decided to do a "one-on-one" approach with only those teachers he felt were more open to new ideas, and again, got nowhere until he met with me. He told me that the chemistry teacher at the nearest girls' school was getting too elderly, and could no longer keep up, so would I consider, just as an initial experiment, taking a batch of say, 20 or so girls as students, along with the usual contingent of boys for the following year in my chemistry classes. I said, "Sure, I'll give it a shot," not realizing at all what I had gotten myself into. At the next faculty meeting, when my decision was announced, the majority of the rest of our faculty looked daggers at me and I was nearly shunned for the remainder of that year.

The following academic year began, with my classes sporting a bright-eyed, excited batch of junior (third year) girls which I welcomed and worked into my seating arrangement with a roughly equal number of boys. It turned out that this group of girls were not only unusually pretty, as a group, but were quite bright, as well, and soon gave the boys all the grade competition they could handle. That whole first, partially coed year I was regularly grilled by the other faculty members as to what it was like to have girls in my class, and I had to admit that in many ways it was an improvement, since, for one thing, adolescent boys become very self-conscious around pretty girls, even just one, not wanting to appear boorish or stupid, and this made them much easier to deal with. When there is an all-male environment, manners and such tend to deteriorate, and the atmosphere becomes almost military. This is not to say that girls are always perfectly docile, but their ways are usually not so openly, aggressively disobedient, but are more covert, and so, less inflammatory. Indeed, they can be sneaky, catty, even petty, but open hostility, or belligerence is seldom their approach, in my experience. I've never seen a group of girls instigate a food-fight!

After a few months, all of us began to see a noticeable improvement in hall manners and in cafeteria behavior, and soon, most everyone became quite at ease with our radically altered student body dynamics. In addition, as it became apparent that since I had been able to make this work for my own classes, maybe it could work for the whole school. So when that same girls school went "belly-up" financially, our principal, along with the whole administrative team, decided to go coed, and the very next academic year saw us with hundreds of girls in lots of classes school-wide, much to the benefit of our previously dwindling coffers. And how the girls loved it, and never tired of saying so. The older boys pretended to resent it at first, but soon accepted it and found out it wasn't so bad after all. The faculty stopped shunning me and soon forgot that I was the reason it .had all happened in the first place. Another successful "chemistry" experiment! I think our whole faculty had become aware that sometimes change can, indeed, be for the better. The **edge of red** can be a scary place to be at times, but riding it out as we did, it once again paid off.

Chapter 13

The Food Drive

This being a Catholic school, one of its missions, as stated in the student handbook, was to train people who were "people for others," that is, individuals who would want to unselfishly look out for the welfare of those less fortunate than they themselves were. In order to drive home the plight of the needy in the community, for many years this school, just before Thanksgiving, each academic year, had conducted a very successful food drive, wherein the students would be given the task of "begging" a given quota of non-perishable grocery items by evening solicitation throughout the residential neighborhoods of the city. After all, wasn't one of the Christian corporal works of mercy to **feed the hungry?** When I first saw this effort, I was amazed at the utter **scope** of this project. Since the school was all-boys in those days, I was astonished when I first saw the ambitious goals outlined by the principal at the big all-school food drive "kick-off" convocation in the school gym. The goal for the school was 40,000 lbs. of food! I thought to myself,

"There is no way these kids are going to go out there and drum up that much food in two weeks' time. We'll be lucky to see a third of that."

How wrong I was. By the end of that first **academically** disastrous week, they had the lower hall of the building, which was about ten feet wide by half a block in length, full to knee height from one end to the other! I tried my best to get into the spirit that first year, making the case for helping the poor and unfortunate as earnestly as I could, but my homeroom simply was not doing the job. I felt badly for the list of needy families that my room was assigned to feed, for I could see we were not going to have much to distribute. For some reason I just was unable to motivate my kids like many of the other teachers were obviously doing. Come the day of distribution, we put together what we had, divided it up in the cardboard boxes provided by the "campus ministry" group, and our young drivers and their crews took the precious cargoes out to the delighted beneficiaries. We were woefully inadequate, compared to many of the other homerooms, so I vowed to try to find out "how they did it."

("How had all those successful mentors managed to motivate the adolescent male when I apparently could not?")

I didn't want to be too nosy with the faculty, so I began to ask various students who were known to have brought in huge amounts, what it was that had motivated them. After quite a bit of this routine, one kid "let the cat out of the bag"and told me

"You know, Mr. K, maybe you should do like Mr. McGruder. He gives us 10 percent quarter 'A' in his class for every hundred pounds we bring in!" I was shocked, and not a little put out: how **unethical** to hand out unearned grades to kids just to make your own homeroom appear magnanimous! The next year things just got worse. At the end of the first week of the usual two-week quest, the principal could see that the food was not rolling in fast enough for the school to make the yet more ambitious goal that year, so he announced at a faculty meeting,

"Everyone, remember that this is an all-boys school. There is nothing boys like more than a competition, so even though the motivation may not be the ideal, in order to get these kids really going, I am going to accelerate things a bit and announce that for the remainder of this food drive, we will hang up big 'thermometer' posters for each homeroom in the upper hall, and they will continually be updated to show how much food each teacher has gotten in up to that time. We will even work out a set of prizes for the top homeroom and for the top students in each of the four years. Let's see how this works! We've signed up to deliver food to a huge group this year, and we just can't let 'em down."

What a motivator that turned out to be! Now I was being beaten all hollow, and I knew I had to come up with something fast. I have always been a "schemer" by nature, and tapping that resource now, for all I was worth, I came up with a number of effective strategies. One that I remember well was as follows. There was one rather small section of material in my chemistry text which was sort of optional coverage, that is, it was descriptive subject matter that was not strongly emphasized in the end-of-the-year cooperative, "national" exam I always had proudly entered my chem juniors in (and had used to evaluate my own ability in covering chemistry over the previous academic year). Because of the relative unimportance of that section of subject matter, I reasoned, I would present that section, and that section alone during the food drive week, and assign a big test, to be given at the two-weeks' end (as I often did with a given "theory block") but I would simply promise to **let out of that test anyone who would bring in a prescribed amount of food** (knowing inside that that threatened exam was really never planned, or needed to begin with!). That way I had hoped to motivate the kids without giving out unearned grades and without failing to cover the really important subject matter the students would need to master, both to score well on the big final, and, more importantly, to be prepared for further science-related college majors. That turned out to be a brainstorm! The kids fell for it "hook, line and sinker" and that system stood me in good stead for many years, before the school went coed. My homeroom not only became competitive, but began to set record total numbers, both overall, and per-capita, which still stand today. Yes, altruism was eclipsed by competitive fever in the heat of the quest, but each year, at the end of the project, how thrilled we always had become to take voluminous quantities of food to the many worthy recipients. Many times we were nearly brought to tears (boys, yet!) with the shower of thanks these needy folks would give us. It was, for sure, a devious procedure, but I decided to learn to live with it. I am not contending that the end ever justifies the means, but then, I don't claim to be a perfect Christian!

Another incident comes to mind. One year, nearing the end of the drive, I could see that my homeroom was simply not going to be number one this time unless I came up with another bright idea, and quick. My students assured me they had completely "drained dry" their neighborhood resources, and we were at our wits' end, for we needed about another ton to forge into the lead. Suddenly one boy who had been commuting from a local truck farm offered,

"Mr. K, I know they want good produce. My folks have fields of pumpkins, squash and apples. I'll bet I could get them to donate a **truckload** by Friday!"

What a shot in the arm! I said,

"Billy, you might have the answer right there. Go for it!"

Billy was gone the whole next day (Thursday), but on Friday afternoon, we heard, out in the rear of the school, where the big concrete slab was holding the produce portion of the food, the sound of an arriving diesel vehicle. It was Billy, looking proud as punch, with a full **dump truck** of produce, which I found out later he had obtained not only from his folks, but from their neighbors, as well. This turned out to be a staggering weight of stuff, and pushed my homeroom way over the top for that year's contest! My homeroom became famous for its food drive performances, and in this yearly effort, I feel I enhanced my standing with my students, their now knowing that I had other interests in life than just science. My fellow **faculty** members were justifiably not impressed with the method, but because of their guilt over their own schemes, never said much!

After the school went coed (see earlier chapter), I was never again able to produce the big numbers in subsequent food drives, and only managed to hold my own in this project for the remainder of my tenure. In fact, with the new mixed student make-up had come quite a contingent of female faculty, who were not at all convinced that the contest approach was morally healthy. The school totals were destined to dwindle from the outrageous amounts gleaned in the "old days," at least, at first, but we all were eventually won over to a fresh, truly compassionate approach, which, I understand, is still in force nowadays, and finally really working well. The amounts of food gathered by that school every year, and distributed to truly needy folks has been nearly miraculous. In fact I was told just the other day that their last food drive netted them 140,000 lbs., so the compassionate approach is obviously succeeding at last!

Chapter 14

Ya Gotta Love 'em,
and It Helps If You Like 'em, Too.

I had nearly finished handing back a set of corrected lab reports one day, when I detoured to the big cork bulletin board on the north wall of the lab-classroom. I proceeded to tack the last one in my hand up for all to see, and loudly proclaimed, "**Ann, this paper is a masterpiece. The format is perfect, all theory is correctly presented, and your results are just what all groups were striving for. I am going to leave this up here for a few days for everyone to see what a really great lab report can be!**" The girl sat up ramrod straight in her seat, fairly bursting with pride and exhibiting a smile that lit up the room. It really was very well written, so I was merely giving credit where credit was due, but calling public attention to the achievement made all the difference. Ann's work just got better and better from that day forward, and I noticed some of the more serious students looking that paper over between classes.

How delightful high school students can be if they feel they are doing something important, and that they have done it well! If you want what is best for your charges, that is the meaning of real love, and acting daily with that in mind, you will likely begin to really enjoy knowing many of them, and that means you are beginning to **like** them, as well. The former is your duty, the latter is your reward. A few of my fellow teachers regularly talked sarcastically to the students, often engaging in a "can you top this?" routine with them, accompanied by a nervous body language which demonstrated a degree of hostility which can arise when unrealistic expectations are repeatedly dashed by kids who are just being kids. Love 'em every day. They are just children in adults' bodies, and if they know you care about them, that is half the battle. Being **strict** will not destroy their love, but being **mean** or pompous will! Many people never learn the difference between being strict and being mean. If you are mean, the kids will feel you don't love them, much less like them, and the result is disastrous.

Chapter 15

The Science "Un-Fair"

When I was hired on as the new chemistry "prof" at this high school which was to be my place of work for the next thirty-seven years, as it turned out, the two Jesuit priests who showed me around and interviewed me that April day in 1965, made very sure that I well understood that I was to be the very first lay person ever to become a part of their faculty who would not be expected to coach a sport, in addition to teaching a full load. I had also turned down the athletic department's pleas that I coach the boys track team, not because I lacked experience. (In fact, I had been a member of that same school's "cindermen" team myself and had achieved a school letter award for two years of running the hurdles as both a junior and a senior student there.) I had also successfully volunteer-coached track and field, football and basketball at the primary-school level before becoming a certificated teacher. I turned down the coaching job reluctantly, because without the extra pay I would receive for a high-profile extra-curricular such as boys track and field, the salary I would command was practically laughable when compared to what I had been used to in my previous two aerospace engineer/scientist positions, and now with four children to raise, I would need a reasonable income, especially with our (my wife's and my own) unshakable belief that mommy's place was in the home taking care of the children, which commitment my wife bravely stuck with for many years while our children were young. My reluctance to add coaching to my duties, I found out later, had nearly cost me serious consideration for the teaching position in the first place. However, the Jesuits, in those days in a position to expect to get their money's worth out of every lay employee, decided that I could still contribute sufficiently if I would agree to take over the school's science-competition effort and hopefully transform the school's flagging participation in the local science fair event, which they were not prepared to pay a stipend for, but, in which they wanted tangible, visible results! In other words, they wanted to see our students packing home a representative number of prizes and awards!

Remember, this was the "olden days." Catholic schools survived, in large measure because of a huge volume of lay volunteerism. The administrative people of all these schools had become so accustomed to this asset, that, for many years, in the 40's, 50's and 60's, if you were not willing to be involved in volunteering your "time, treasure or talents" for the good of the school of your choice, your children would likely not be granted admission to that school. The demand for these schools was so great during those years that this policy was understood by everyone, and accepted without any resentment. I had always been willing to do my part for the schools my children had attended, volunteer coaching, at different times, track, football and basketball at various schools, and I was very pleased with the education my own children had received in these in-demand schools. Still, these schools up to that time were mainly staffed by men and women of religious orders, who had, by virtue of a vow of poverty, exempted themselves from union salary bargaining, with the horrendous financial burden on the school that the greatly increased salaries would inevitably impress. This system had worked famously for a couple of decades, turning these schools into family affairs, supplying all concerned with a sense of true mission that is difficult to portray through the printed word alone. The atmosphere of these places was just as wonderful as a given faculty had the "moxie" to make it. The dedication of this school's alumni and parents' organization had always been legend, and a teacher or coach here could always count on the support of the community in nearly every way, at least in the "old days."

Therefore, I felt very fortunate to find myself chosen to fill the position as chemistry teacher, and gladly accepted the science fair advocate job, rather than taking on a task like athletic team coaching, which I had refused because I doubted I could handle the workload. Actually, it was rare to see a chemistry or physics teacher in high school also acting as a coach of a major team sport, because of the tremendous amount of after-class time needed to prepare laboratory sessions. Although this was a given, the Catholic schools were slow to accept this concept, and this administration found this "bitter pill" a little easier to swallow with my acceptance of the role of science competition director.

It turned out that this job was to be a much bigger challenge than anyone could have expected! For one thing the school had no tradition of excellence in this particular area, meaning that I would be starting from scratch in my attempt to build a competitive program. In addition, the Catholic (parochial) school system which fed students to this high school had not carried any such program, either, so that unlike the public school system, where this sort of competition was sponsored and strongly encouraged practically from first grade, our students were "as green as grass" when they arrived on our campus. Our principal at that time, though very intelligent and dedicated to overall academic excellence (as I mention below in a later chapter), was uneasy, even suspicious, at first, of what he thought was the "materialistic" bent of the whole scientific approach to problem-solving. It was obvious to me that if I was to get the school really going on this project, I would need to win him over, since the whole-hearted support of this guy was essential to the success of any program in this school.

Once I achieved a reasonable level of comfort in my classroom courses, I decided to "kick off" a science fair competition program, but, to my disappointment, my first attempt to arouse interest in science project work fell on deaf ears. Now I can see why. You'll remember what an unsuccessful first year my chemistry classes were. It was actually so bad, as I have explained, that I was nearly fired after that first year. I am sure now that there was no interest in my big plans because I simply had not yet achieved enough respect to inspire any confidence in prospective participants. Trying again, well into what was turning out to be a much better, second year for me, I instigated an after-school "science club" which was offered to any and all students with possible science-career interests. At this point in time I had not yet started the ham radio program, so a fair amount of my after-school time was available for this activity. The turn-out was pretty good, with about seven or eight boys showing up. Keep in mind, we were still an all-boys school at that time, and I began to organize the first "club" of this type ever on this campus.

These were high quality, very good students, eager to learn more about science and engineering careers, and I proceeded to set up elections to choose club officers. Next we decided on subsequent meeting times, after which I began to bring in science movies and invited numerous guest speakers from local college engineering and science schools, to which a portion of every week's time would be devoted. Finally, I broached the inevitable subject, the reason for our existence: our hopeful participation in the all-district science fair in the spring. Everyone wanted to give it a try, but none of us had any useful experience. I purchased a few paperbacks on the subject and each boy picked a project from the lists upon which he would work, hoping to wind up with something that would be worthy of entry in the spring.

Come spring we managed to come up with a few entries, mostly models, some working, some not, of historically famous landmark scientific devices. None of them garnered more than a certificate of participation, so it was "back to the drawing boards" for evaluation of our prowess, or lack thereof.

We all noticed that those projects which had won prizes were nearly all research-oriented, which none of ours had been. Thus it was that I did a complete rethink of the whole enterprise and decided finally to reorganize everything. Starting the following year, I dropped the "science club" moniker altogether, calling the activity "advanced science." I saw to it that it became a full credit, after regular class-hours science **course**, and was able to fill its ranks with senior students, by invitation only, who had excelled in my earlier chemistry class, as juniors. Since we were now coed, I began to get about an equal mix of boys and girls, and the quality improved noticeably because this was now respected as a true "honors"-type academic class, rather than merely an after-school "club" for science nerds! Another brainstorm really launched us: each student would be expected to choose a scientific research-type project, and it would count a sizable portion of the course's grade. Grading would be based on such considerations as originality, timeliness, difficulty, and presentation. If good enough, we would enter it in the fair in the spring. In addition to the project aspect of the course, I chose a number of recently important "industrial" scientific topics upon which to lecture. (I was well aware of many, since I had just been immersed in the aerospace industry for five years before entering teaching). I covered things like thermodynamics, cryogenics, high temperature materials technology, and after I obtained my Master's degree at Purdue University, in 1970, I was able to add organic chemistry and analytical chemistry. Later on, as I began to teach a separate class in electronics (see chapter 23, "Hamming it up," below), I added a section on "electronics for scientists." This new approach turned out to be a winner, as I'll explain, but trouble was still in store for our group of would-be scientists.

This program, as a bona-fide class, became wildly successful, with more outstanding applicants every year than I could incorporate in the class. Soon, very large percentages of our very best graduates were choosing and succeeding in science and science-related majors in prestigious universities all over the country. One or two years after this program was initiated, over 90 percent of our top seniors were becoming physicians, dentists, engineers and scientists, much to my satisfaction, even though there was some resentment arising in other faculty members as their prospects for such stand-byes as fine-arts, journalism and debate electives began to choose the "advanced science" alternative instead, making it difficult for these teachers of other advanced electives to find qualified students.

I (along with the science program in general) was enjoying all this newly appearing popularity, and everything would have been perfect except for one little problem: we still could not seem to win major, school-district-awarded prizes at the science fair! We had begun to do very well with those prizes awarded by the military services and especially with those given by the national scientific societies, but were routinely ignored by the judges from the local district, whose favor alone, it turned out, was essential if one of our students was to move on with his or her project to national competition. We "rolled with the punches" for a couple more years, until one year we had an entry that I felt was a sure winner. This boy, Paul, had carried out an intricately planned chemistry research project which was based on an idea I myself had had years before when I was doing high temperature intermetallic compounds development at LLNL in California. Not only had he, with my tutoring (he had done all the actual hands-on work), made an actual chemical discovery, but, being a very accomplished debater, he was able to explain masterfully to the entire panel of judges, almost perfectly, the whole project, including possible future applications of the find. When Paul finished his outstanding presentation, I noticed the judges from the American Chemical Society applauding and I was convinced for a second we would finally win the "sweepstakes" prize. But it was not meant to be. To my utter dismay, the district judges disqualified Paul's project, on the grounds that it was "too large" to be sent to the national competition! Instead, they awarded the prize to a boy (and I still remember this vividly) who claimed to have created a controversial substance, called "polywater." I was well versed in this "polywater" concept, since for years the scientific journals had been filled with articles submitted by chemists all over the world who, at that moment in history, had claimed to have seen evidence of this polymeric form of water. What led me to doubt this boy's work was the sheer amount of the substance he claimed to have prepared. If this little tube of stuff was really polywater, this boy would be displaying more of the precious liquid than existed in all the laboratories of the world! A little later the polywater concept was debunked when x-ray diffraction specialists and other analytical chemists proved that this purported new, amazing form of water was nothing more than sodium silicate, called "water glass" in years gone by, a substance sometimes leached from glass containers under certain conditions. Needless to say, this poor lad's project, when shown at the national science fair competition (that year in Minneapolis, I believe), was not a serious contender, and, in addition, no more articles were appearing in the journals on this fabled substance they had called "polywater"! I had to feel sorry for the misguided lad who had mistakenly been initially covered with false glory, at the expense of our legitimate scientist-orator, Paul.

About a week after this traumatic science fair, I got a phone call from the guy who was the chairman of the local science fair committee. I'll never forget his exact words, which were,

"Kurt, you guys were screwed, I know. The project that went back east last year was bigger than Paul's! I have a proposition for you: how would you like to come and take over my job for next year? I'm running out of steam, having done this now for the better part of a decade, plus we need some new blood on the committee, and you seem to have developed a pretty good handle on what is needed to produce outstanding science projects."

I was absolutely furious, and said to him

69

"What you are really saying, Frank, is that if I want my students to have a chance of one day winning a sweepstakes prize, I'll need to be on the committee, right?"

"That's about it," he replied.

My response was,

"You know what you can do with this so-called science fair!"

Then and there I proceeded to discontinue our participation in that science fair competition (along with ten or fifteen other schools who had been noticing similar shenanigans for some time). For lack of interest the fair itself was dropped shortly thereafter.

That student, Paul, went on, with a good scholarship, to obtain his degree in electrical engineering, and next secured a fine position as an R&D engineer with the Hewlett-Packard Corporation, I was pleased to see. Fortunately, he never allowed his bad experience to embitter him.

After that time, we continued with the projects, but if a project seemed outstanding enough, I would try to supply as much information to the student as I could find to allow the student to enter his or her project in whatever national competitions of the type were available at the time, such as the "Westinghouse Science Talent Search" and others. However, the wind had gone out of my sails for all-out assaults on high-profile award quests. Since no other of our science faculty was ever to show serious interest in such an endeavor, this school never did achieve the kind of "fame" that had been envisioned by that group of Jesuit administrators, ten years earlier! That failed effort has always been one of the few regrets I have had in all those years of high school teaching, although I realize now that that aspect was actually only unimportant "window-dressing" when compared to the much more significant fact of the dozens of scientific and engineering career choices engendered by that "advanced science" program over the years.

I do feel, as well, that all that intense, competitive effort during those "science-fair" years enhanced my own teaching "edge" by causing me to be more alert to the latest discoveries in many areas of current scientific work. **Science** teaching is especially dependent on continuous maintenance of up-to-date knowledge of the state of the art in the specific subject area one has specialized in (in my case, chemistry, and later electronics, as well). Kept me again on that very important **edge of red!**

Chapter 16

The Self-Esteem Game

One day, after classes, I was in my room still, preparing a chemical demonstration for the next day's classes, as I often did for an hour or two after the last class of the day, when in sauntered a couple of my students, one of whom seemed eager to get my attention, to ask a question. He blurted out something like,

"Mr. K, I think you gave me too low a grade on my last lab report. It was extremely well written, and I think I was robbed! I would put it up against any of the others."

His friend looked a little chagrined, but waited around to see my response. I replied matter-of-factly,

"Mr. Wilkerson, your ability is exceeded only by your humility."

Wilkerson looked puzzled, until his buddy broke into hysterical laughter and said to Wilkerson,

"You've just been insulted, you know."

After that we had a brief discussion of what it would take to have achieved a higher grade on that paper, and I never did have to explain the "insult" which had been really totally spontaneous and unplanned on my part. I felt a bit guilty about it afterwards, because it was my policy never to put down a student, and I still feel that is the best policy. Nevertheless, it is fashionable in educational circles to blame "a lack of self-esteem" for bad behavior exhibited by a given student, and, indeed, this can often be the case. Unfortunately, the exact opposite can cause problems, as well, as the above example illustrates, but this imbalance is oddly ignored by most educators. Children of doting, over-solicitous parents often become so "full of themselves" that they are unable to admit that they don't know it all, that they may be in need of advice. In my experience, too much false (engendered) self esteem is just as big a hindrance to true emotional and intellectual growth as is too little of the commodity. True self esteem is the natural result of the knowledge of a job well-done, and, given lots of opportunities, students of all backgrounds, colors and nationalities will usually find something they can excel at. I have seen it happen over and over again, and it was for the thrill of seeing it happen that I gladly gave up a rocket scientist's salary and status and never seriously, for any length of time, regretted doing so.

Chapter 17

The Rotten Smell of Success

Chemistry laboratories always develop a characteristic odor all their own. Whenever, in later years, someone who had been my student years before, would come to visit me, upon their entry to my classroom, they would always exclaim something like, "Ahh, the fragrance of the chem lab!" The odor of burning sulfur (mostly just sulfur dioxide) along with hints of chlorine gas, ammonia gas, and a myriad of other volatiles combine, the world over, to produce a very clinging smell that distinguishes a chemistry laboratory immediately from any other venue. I had worked in such labs for so many years, even by the time I was just beginning my teaching career, that the "lab fragrance" was all but nonexistent to me. I think my olfactory senses had been numbed to the point of inability even to detect this particular odor.

There is, however, one smell which adds itself to the composite, which by itself is so objectionable that it offends me even to this day: the notorious odor of hydrogen sulfide gas, that well-known "rotten-egg" smell, which is produced by any number of common general chemistry reactions, and, unfortunately must needs be generated from time to time in the course of any comprehensive general chemistry class. Lay people often mistake hydrogen sulfide for the much less offensive sulfur dioxide; but in any case, both of these gases can be toxic in strong concentrations. I was well aware of the need to prevent build-up of these gases in the classroom. Noticing that the room's little exhaust fan would be woefully inadequate, I requested installation of a better one, which was soon done. Oh, what a fan that new one was! When we turned it on, during lab sessions, the roar drowned out my voice so thoroughly I was forced to install a p.a. system and from then on I sported a little shirt-collar mounted wireless microphone on lab days. Also (and I am not making this up), when someone with long hair would mosey by in the hall and look in, their hair would be drawn into the room, along with any hat that might have been worn! It was a hilarious side-effect, but along with the fan roar, it served to add even more to the repute of the infamous Kromholtz chem lab. Even hydrogen sulfide, which had plagued the lives of this school's earlier chem teachers and had brought me my share of derogatory comments from other faculty members and administrators as well, was no longer a problem. I could now allow some of the gas to be generated and could eliminate the odor with impunity. (This was especially useful in the inorganic cation qualitative analysis section of my newly formed and well-attended "advanced chemistry" class for outstanding career-minded seniors.) That fan turned over the air so well in that lab-classroom that, once it was installed, I never again got a complaint from anyone about objectionable odors. The really amazing thing was that the students themselves began even to "like" the sulfurous odor of the chem lab. In fact, in the halls of the school, I would often run into one of my ex-chem students, now a senior and taking physics, who would tell me he or she truly missed the odors of chemistry! They say that the olfactory senses are the senses most closely tied to human memory, and I could only gather from this that most of their memories of my class must have been good ones. As the years went by and I began to teach the children of my earlier students, their parents, during PTA conferences would recall those "bad odors" with fond, nostalgic reminiscences, and this happened so often, I knew it was sincere. The only reservations I had were my concern about the way the kids had smelled when they had returned home from my class. I'll bet that was not so well-received, but that's one of the many charms of chemistry!

Chapter 18

Tell 'em a Story

"Mike! Hold it! Stop what you're doing right there!
Everyone, listen up! Put down your equipment and pay close
attention to me. We nearly had a disaster here! I want you all to
look up at the ceiling just above Bill's and Molly's desk. Can you
all see the black mess there?

"For many years I have deliberately asked the janitorial
people who would normally clean that sort of stuff up, to leave it
there as a reminder of a near-disaster we once had when a couple of
my students, Gary Masterson and Philip Crandall *[I used the actual
names at the time]* forgot, as Mike and Louise here just did, to wait
the required ten seconds before lighting the end of the hydrogen
delivery tube. As you may remember from our pre-lab discussion,
when that happens, and we therefore have both hydrogen and air

coming out, the flame can go back through the delivery tube into the flask itself, and blow up. Fortunately, Gary and his partner did remember to first wrap up the generator flask with toweling, so that the chemicals and glass were forced to go nowhere but straight up to the ceiling producing the black blotches you can all see there still years later! This sort of thing can happen to anyone. We've seldom had a serious accident in this lab, mainly because I always watch you all so carefully, but there's always that element of danger in a chem lab experiment, and the ability to control these potentially dangerous experiments will give you the confidence to handle college lab work of any kind.

"Now, let's go over the correct procedure once again, then we'll do the hydrogen blow-torch experiment with more confidence."

The kids were riveted as they heard this tale of near disaster, and for a short while they probably would have believed anything I had told them. They then proceeded to carry out the experiment with great excitement, and without mishap. Some students confided in me later that that day's lab was the most exciting experience they had ever had in high school.

Over the years I built up quite a repertoire of true stories which, after I embellished 'em for dramatic effect, served to spice up my lecture-discussion sessions, especially during pre-lab preparation periods. I discovered that much more interest always resulted when I used names of the actual students in the stories, but I never did so without first checking with those students to get their permission to do so. High school students like notoriety almost as much as fame, provided they are not made to appear "dorky" (or stupid) in the telling. They crave attention, above all.

Here's a true story which I related to my classes every year, early in the year, to make the very real dangers of careless behavior with chemicals prominent in their young, enthusiastic minds, hopefully mitigating any over-blown anticipation of the glamour and excitement of explosive chemical combinations. One of our elderly religion teachers had told me this story, in great detail in the faculty lounge, at break one day, even naming the unfortunate student, and that of the responsible chemistry teacher (now replaced by me, of course). It turns out that this "chem prof" had been in the habit of running numerous student lab sessions devoted to the examination of the explosive properties of a group of elements called the "alkali metals." These include, among others, sodium, potassium and lithium. These have many similar, fascinating properties. They are so soft that they can be "cut with a knife," they oxidize in the air, and, most interestingly, they all react explosively with water (that is, they need to be stored under oil or kerosene, since any contact with water, even water vapor, can cause an explosion. It turns out that this chemistry teacher had been passing out considerable quantities of the least expensive (most plentiful) of these "alkali" metals, namely **sodium** metal to the students in his lab classes one year, every day, for about a week, and leading them through a set of interesting reactions designed to show the chemical similarities of this well-known active metal group. One aggressive, opportunistic lad had decided to purloin a marble-sized piece of the magic metal and had stuffed it in his front pants-pocket when the teacher's head was turned. During the mid-morning recess period, as most of the male students did in the fall of the year, he had decided to get involved in a quick pick-up game of intramural touch football, where he played vigorously for the full fifteen minutes allotted, then scurried to his next class, grabbing his text and barely making it before the bell rang, starting his 3rd year religion class, where he was immediately expected to quietly pay close attention to, and take notes for the teacher who was now telling me this tale. Suddenly, the astonished lad leaped out of his lecture-chair wildly slapping at his pant-leg, where flames were flashing upwards! This teacher explained to me that he had instantly handed an empty coffee cup to another student, urging him to run to the hall to a drinking fountain for water to douse these flames, and the student did so, with great efficiency, but when they dumped the water, with great initial relief, on the burning spot of the boy's pants, lo and behold, the fire only got worse!!! By now the boy was in agony, and, tearing off the pant leg, he could see a horrible, festering wound in the boy's leg. It was no longer flaming, but seemed to be "fizzing" much like an alka-seltzer tablet in water. A student handed the panicking teacher his handkerchief, and he scrubbed out the wound as best he could, dislodging the frothing piece of oddly shiny foreign material, then smothering the wound with lots and lots of petroleum jelly from his desk drawer. I was absolutely flabbergasted at this story, and, being a chemist, I knew immediately what had happened. The hunk of sodium, heretofore resting so benignly in the pocket of the young thief, had found itself subjected to the considerable water content of the perspiration generated by the unwitting, profusely sweating football player, and had only done what it had to do, namely react violently, producing lots of heat—but also another product, **sodium hydroxide**. This is known as **lye**, an even more toxic, well-known, caustic substance in its own right. As the burning sodium metal ate its way into his leg, it would have reacted further with the water in his blood, creating more flames, and even more lye, which would have aggravated everything beyond measure! It's no wonder the added water did not help anything, since water was the culprit to begin with! Being a true story, I found this one always another spellbinder, and have told it "early and often" over the years.

Chapter 19

"Hats Off" to Respect

Teenagers are capable of a seemingly unending variety of transgressions. One year, for many reasons, the school atmosphere had been degrading for a good while, Such "small" behavior problems as blatant littering, use of bad language, bullying, and tardiness were all on the rise, in the classrooms as well as elsewhere. Even the most liberal members of the faculty were becoming appalled. Nearly every faculty meeting, no matter the original discussion topic, would soon revert to earnest questions as to how to improve the increasingly hostile atmosphere. Our principal initiated a very structured, sanction-based new approach, which helped temporarily, at least to the extent that he could get the faculty "on board." After a while, it became obvious that this "band-aid," authoritative system was not going to be enough, because when one type of misbehavior was quelled, soon the kids would creatively come up with another we hadn't even thought of. Clearly there was some underlying problem which needed to be exposed, then dealt with, on some psychological level.

One day we had a real brainstorm. During a "forum" type session in a faculty meeting, suddenly an elderly, beloved Jesuit priest (who had taught religion and English for many years) yelled out, "What is it with all these kids wearing hats, all over the school nowadays, even in the classrooms? I don't see it, at all!" The room went dead silent. It was as though all the frustration we had all been feeling had been summed up in that one statement. No more was said about that particular topic, at that meeting, but two or three days later, our usually rather timid school lay president issued a proclamation to the whole school which read, "Henceforth all students and faculty are to remove their hats when entering the school building. Wearing of hats anywhere in the school building shall be considered disrespectful, and will be treated as such by all faculty and administrators." For about two weeks or so, there were a few violations, and even the president himself could be seen occasionally knocking a hat off the head of some unwary student. The students, especially the seniors, at first pretended to resent the rule, but before long bought into it, and you cannot believe the change that this brought over the whole school atmosphere. Loud burping was dying out, public displays of affection became rare, and bullying was now looked down upon. I was so impressed by the courage displayed by our little president, and told him so. The seniors even dedicated their beloved yearbook that year to the "hats off" theme.

School pride showed a noticeable resurgence, and school discipline was much less work for us all. I really think that right then and there, had the administrative team been so inclined, they could have required the students to wear **uniforms** and the kids would have loved the idea, because it would have said to the public, "See who we are? We are proud of who we are!" I always felt it was a sadly missed opportunity, but there are many who would disagree with a "dinosaur" like me.

Chapter 20

The Principal is Your Pal

Once I had completed my work at the University of Washington, just after the big aerospace layoff I spoke of earlier, had forced me into a career decision, in order to obtain a little income while I searched for a permanent chemistry teaching position, I spent most of the following year doing substitute teaching at literally dozens of junior and senior high schools in the huge Seattle "Metro" school district. I started this interim work with some apprehension, since I had heard all sorts of dire advice, both from teachers and others. I remember one day, strolling onto a big Seattle high school campus, and one of the regular faculty asking me "

"Are you the new sub for so-and-so today? Where's your baseball bat?"

However, for the most part this turned out to be a useful experience for me since it provided me an opportunity to observe and evaluate the performance of a host of schools, utilizing a variety of educational approaches, and to do so from a rather disinterested, that is, open-minded, view-point. One major item I noticed, again and again, was how critically important to the success of the school was the quality of that school's principal. In practically every case, if you showed me a school where the head man was intelligent, up-front, dedicated and upright, I would show you a school with a focused student body, a cooperative, optimistic faculty and successful academic and even athletic programs. In some schools, however, it seemed to me that the faculty subscribed to a "don't rock the boat" philosophy, wherein the "teachers pretended to teach and the students pretended to learn." This "a happy kid in a happy classroom" approach gave an outward appearance of a successful program, but I was always asking myself, "were these students being adequately prepared for their futures?" Although handing out candy-coated A's reduced strife temporarily, later down the road, would the students be able to cope with the competition to be reckoned with both in college and in the work place? I thought not.

When I first began in my career position I was fortunate to be blessed with an outstanding principal. (In fact, he had been involved in hiring me.) He was a middle-aged Jesuit priest who had only held the job for a couple of years prior to my arrival. He didn't seem to be well-liked, and I soon learned that he had replaced a man who had been a legend at that school, for many, many years. (He had been principal when I was a **student** there!) He was loved, even revered by most of the faculty, but was forced to retire due to failing health. This new guy was, I had to admit, not the "hail-fellow-well-met" type. Rather cool and reserved, he was a masterful guy who said what he meant, meant what he said, and you had better "be on board," or you would hear from him. He had a very clear vision of what he wanted the school to be and he made it a point to know absolutely everything that was going on around the school, at all times. "Touchy-feely" he was not, but he was so honest, so intelligent and so forthright that he won me over right away. Actually, he was so vigorous and competent, that I was "spoiled" by those few early years when he was my "boss," and the five subsequent administrations I worked under always seemed inadequate to me, probably because they seemed to pale by comparison. Also, as a substitute teacher I had seen many other principals in action, thus I felt I had the background to spot prowess at the position when I saw it!

It was this fellow who forced me to the single biggest turning point in my teaching career. When my disastrous first year was over, he invited me to confer with him in his office, and when he realized that I was not even aware that my approach had been "breeding" discipline problems, he said to me (burning words I still remember, verbatim, to this day),

"Kurt, you have the makings of a fine teacher, I think, but unless you are willing to change an approach which is creating behavior problems, I'm not going to be able to renew your contract for next year."

The words hit me like a kick in the stomach, but part of me knew he was right and all I could do was stammer back,

"Okay, what would you suggest I do?"

He proceeded to give me some tips, including one which I thought was in jest, at first. He actually told me,

"If I were you, I would not smile the first day."

He also suggested that I give the class a layout, at the very start, of my major expectations of them as regards their behavior. He said this should be done with specific detail concerning possible, typical infractions which could ensue and how such infractions would be dealt with. But he let me have another year at it, and employing most of his suggestions (including the "no-smile first day" warning). I immediately saw a tremendous improvement in my classes, making my second year finally a reasonably satisfying experience. Later that second year when he and I were once again conferring about various issues, I remember him saying to me,

"Kurt, I am in no sense a scientist."

I still regret that I did not have the presence of mind to reply,

"Father, I've worked under you for more than a year now, and I've noticed that when you come across a method that works, you hold on to it, and even promote it, yet when you encounter another system or plan which doesn't, you drop it. Now, that's the scientific method, if I've ever seen it!"

Unfortunately, however, I had missed a good opportunity to compliment a special man, a truly masterly administrator, in a totally honest way, and never got another such opportunity. By being completely honest and firm with me, he had salvaged a flagging career, and this principal, therefore, had actually been my pal, after all!

Chapter 21

The All-Important Sense of Humor

High school students, as I am fond of saying, rarely have yet lost their sense of humor, and it is in large measure this fact which initially attracted me to teaching at this level. With a subject as mentally demanding as chemistry, a little comic relief is always much appreciated by the students, and **once the respect is there**, humor can be effectively injected from time to time with impunity. It became a staple portion of my delivery, especially when I found it strengthened my point on a certain methodology. Literally hundreds of examples come to mind, but this one is representative: It had been my policy, near the end of each academic year, to devote two or three classes to lab apparatus drawer clean-up, and inventory. The procedure would work like this: each twosome would remove their drawer from the desk, take out all apparatus and glassware, clean it all and check it against a supplied inventory sheet. Once they felt they were finished cleaning and replenishing the drawer, they would call over a lab assistant for an "okay," then sign the back of the sheet, put it in the drawer, replace the drawer in the desk and get it locked up for use of the incoming partnership the next fall. For the purpose of double-checking everyone's work on this important end-of-the year ritual I would always return to the lab-room one or two days during the summer while school was out and make sure the drawers really were ready for another year. One summer I was going through the drawers in this way when I came to one drawer with an unsigned final inventory sheet, and I could see why. That particular partnership had decided to smuggle a message to the incoming twosome. It said, (I am relating this, verbatim, from memory, as I write this)

"You poor sons of **b*****s**, you should have taken **bio**. Inside of two weeks, you are going to be up to your ears in so much **b*******,** you won't know which end is up!"

I have rarely laughed any harder, and never have tired of telling this at cocktail parties, since. My teacher cronies enjoy hearing it all over again, every year. (I swear ,I get asked to tell it.) I decided to tell this story to my students as part of a carefully planned early-in-the-year pep talk, which many would need, because of their early struggles with the rigors of the daunting vocabulary of beginning general chemistry. If you can laugh at **yourself**, you have a handle on the situation, to be sure!

Chapter 22

Sweat the "Little Things"

"Why do you suppose the amount of oxygen in our air remains almost constant at roughly 21%, no matter where you are on the earth's surface, even while the rain forests, as some claim, are rapidly disappearing due to uncontrolled development?"

I often kicked-off a class by posing a question to see if anyone had read ahead in the current chapter, or had any real insights. Before I could even scan my class, one girl blurted out loudly, "The oxygen content of our air is determined by the amount of ultraviolet light striking water vapor at the edge of our atmosphere, not by the comparatively paltry amount of the precious gas given off by vegetation or plankton." The class was stunned by the answer, and went dead silent, because the answer was not only marvelously correct and superbly stated, but was obviously done so out of turn. I simply stated,

"Francine, well said, but I want you to join me here right after school this evening to do a little clean-up work. You know better than to speak out without raising your hand for me to recognize you first!"

This particular infraction would happen once or twice, early every year in each and every one of my classes, and some students were always surprised at first to see how big a thing I made out of what seemed to them a minor break in protocol, especially when they had come from one or more classes where that sort of chaotic discourse was tolerated. However, I found very early on that if such "small" infractions were shown to be simply unacceptable, soon class-time give-and-take became a very satisfying experience for both me and for the students, in every class. Also, and more importantly, students then would rarely escalate to more serious behavior problems. Let the poor manners ride, and soon some kid might find himself suspended from school, expelled, or even facing jail time due to hitting a faculty member or some other, much worse act. By being strict as regards the small things we do the kids a tremendous favor, in the long run. Kids feel secure when they know their limits and will not hold this approach against you at all if you are fair, firm and consistent.

Chapter 23

"Hamming It Up"

All teachers, and I think chemistry teachers in particular, are terrible show-offs, by nature. Now that I look back, it was that "fault" which was motivating my little chemical magic show offerings, back when I was just a 10 year old kid. When I was doing high-temperature chemistry research and development work, first for the Atomic Energy Commission (LLNL's "Project Pluto," a nuclear ramjet) in Livermore, and later for an aerospace company in Seattle, both for NASA's "Dyna-Soar" (the original space shuttle) and the "Saturn-5" rocket booster (the biggest and most powerful booster rocket ever used, which ultimately put Neil Armstrong and his cohorts on the moon in the "Apollo" moonshot program), nothing gave me more pleasure than when we would have an interested visitor and I would be asked to explain my work. I would also feel that welcome little shot of extra adrenaline whenever, as a teacher, my classes might be observed by the principal or other administrator. I guess it is the actor in me demanding to emerge, and I think it was that need which prevented me from finding real satisfaction in the field of research. That feature of my personality stood me in good stead for many years, as strictly a teacher of chemistry, but was destined to contribute to yet another major change in my career, after roughly my first decade of teaching. I had been pursuing home entertainment electronics, as a hobby, and had managed, through a correspondence course with Bell & Howell Schools' DeVry Institute, to obtain credentials as a color television repair technician, fixing all sorts of sets to augment the small salary I had been getting as a private school teacher. One day as I was ransacking my little self-appropriated "repair shop" (a small school room which was formerly used as storage for old physics/electronic equipment), looking for a tool of some kind, I came across two large, very well preserved pieces of "ancient" electronic equipment that I knew had belonged to an old Jesuit priest who had been a "ham radio operator." Along with these gadgets was a pile of manuals, logbooks, and bins of assorted parts and tools. I remember thinking, "What a waste! This equipment looks to be still usable. I wonder what this 'ham radio' stuff is all about, and if we could find someone willing to help us get a program like this off the ground again." So in my spare time I perused the documents and manuals left by the old priest who had attempted to start such a program, just a short while before I had come to this school. I found his name from one of his manuals, and ascertained his address and phone number from our principal. In talking to him I found that he himself was not interested in working with high school kids any more, as his experience with them in the past had not been a happy one, but he put me in touch with a layman who, he felt, might just be interested in helping me to get something going. This older gentleman, Rich, turned out to be one of the most wonderful guys you'd ever meet. He was a semi-retired ex military communications expert, himself a licensed amateur radio operator for many years, now working part-time as an electronics office equipment salesman, who told me he'd be glad to do a presentation on "ham" (amateur) radio for a group of interested teenagers at the school. I then set up a date with Rich and next proceeded to put into our "daily bulletin" (read to the whole school every afternoon right after the last class of the day), a message which read something like "Special presentation on Ham Radio, Tuesday evening at 7 p.m. in Room 79 (chemistry lab). All interested welcome to attend. No obligation of any kind." That evening I, along with two of my own sons, one of which was already into the hobby, showed up to be greeted with a turnout of about ten students, all boys of ages from 14 to 18 years. Rich gave an excellent presentation, explaining in detail, all the wondrous things one could do as a radio ham. When the meeting was over almost all of the boys had signed up for more learning, plus, to my delight, my youngest son, who, until that night had not shown much interest in the pursuit, even with constant urging from his already licensed brother. I, personally, was also fascinated, but declined to sign up because I wasn't sure I could learn the five word per minute Morse code requirement, in force at that time, to satisfy the Federal Communications Commission's requirements for their "Novice" (beginner's) Class License. After all, wasn't I 40 years old? I wasn't sure this "old dog" could still learn new tricks! But my youngest son, then only eleven years old, easily passed his code test, and then said, "Dad, if I can do it, you sure can!" I gave it a shot, passed with ease, and then proceeded to read everything I could find to prepare for the Novice Class **written** test, which my young son and I both passed on the same day. My only daughter, my oldest son, and my wife were still holdouts at that point in time. After that I began to schedule regular weekly "ham radio club" meetings, and my two ham sons and I would attend, with Rich lecturing each time on some further facet of this "New World" of Amateur Radio which was opening up before us. The radio club idea really "caught on" and after a few years we were turning out licensed teenage ham radio operators of both sexes, eventually, at the rate of 6 or 8 each year. In addition, the club began to participate in various national operating contests and for three years running garnered the award titled "Top Scoring High School Amateur Radio Club in America" in the big yearly nation-wide "Field Day Emergency Preparedness Contest" put on by the American Radio Relay League (the **ARRL**, America's own organization totally dedicated to the promotion of Amateur Radio), getting us a magazine article or two in the process.

Meanwhile, things were changing a little in society, in those days (the '70s), and the state had put forth a new requirement that all high school graduates must have taken and passed at least a two credit class in **vocational education**. At that point in time the school could only come up with **typing** and **home economics** as satisfactory offerings, and more similar classes were sorely and immediately needed. The principal called me to meet with him in his office and said to me,

"Kurt, we understand that you have now some expertise in electronics, I know you do the ham radio thing, and do you still repair TV's and stereos and such?"

I had to admit he was right on both counts, but what did he have in mind? Then he asked if I might consider teaching a class in electronics to help the school maintain state accreditation. He assured me that the school would provide the necessary equipment, and since the numbers of students enrolling in chemistry were decreasing a little lately, he didn't think another class would add too much to my work load. I was excited to try this, since ham radio had really piqued my interest in radio electronics, and the brand new field of digital electronics was just coming on the scene with magazine articles galore furnishing interesting "lounge reading" for what non-social free time I had been able to find. Thus I was able to add electronics to my class schedule, and the ham radio program was easily integrated into it, providing not only more vocational credit offerings for the school, but firming up and validating the ham radio program as much more than the "club" it had started out to be. This venture into the world of electronics would eventually (many years down the road) be of vastly more importance to me, personally, than I could have imagined at the time; I'll elaborate on this later in this book.

It soon turned out that ham radio was to provide an even more prolific outlet for the show-off side of me. "Gee Whiz" stuff was always happening. One time I took a group of electronics students to the ham room, and calling "CQ," snagged a fellow transmitting from the island of Guam, yet, and it turned out, one of his best friends was teaching at this very school! I sent a kid to this teacher's class and soon Joe was "on the air" yakking with his old college buddy, much to the delight of my student-observers.

Another time, using an "OSCAR" (Orbiting Satellite Carrying Amateur Radio), I was able to talk to operators in Finland and Germany while the impressed students looked on. I even made contacts with a fellow in **Antarctica**, and, one time, using Morse code (or **CW** as the hams refer to it) talked with a youngster who was using a little home-made "sardine-can" transmitter in the Amazon jungles.

Probably the most spectacular accomplishment I ever had with ham radio, however, had nothing to do with school teaching. In the late 70's my only daughter (herself now a ham, as are all of my family) was becoming very proficient in classical ballet, and when she was a high school senior she won a scholarship to dance with the Joffrey Ballet Co. in New York City. I was thrilled, of course, for her achievement, but was a little nervous about my one and only little daughter traveling all that way, so night after night I began trying to find an active ham in or near New York City. Calling "CQ New York City," I soon found **Joe** in Merrick, Long Island, New York! Joe found the story very interesting, and when my daughter landed at La Guardia Airport, he and his Japanese wife were there to meet her, then chauffeured her and her little traveling companion-girlfriend to the special, protected girls' dorm in Manhattan, where she would stay for a couple of years while training for the Joffrey. And for months after that, every Saturday evening her still-attentive boyfriend would come to our home, where we would all gather around my ham station and we would all get a chance to talk to my homesick daughter via **transcontinental** phone patch, courtesy of my newly found New Yorker friend, Joe! We were financially strapped in those days, so the free hookup provided by two ham radio operators was most welcome, indeed. Another interesting application of this technology involved our school club's participation in community events, such as helping to coordinate the city's annual Lilac Festival Armed Forces Day Parade, and the Bloomsday Run. In addition, occasionally I was able to volunteer the kids' technical services for help with providing badly needed communications during times of local disasters, such as "Firestorm '97" or the Mt. St. Helens eruption of 1980. Hams pride themselves as being oftentimes the only still-working method of communication available to a devastated, fearful public, desperate to inform loved ones of their plight. That is why it is called the "Ham Radio **Service**," rather than only a hobby.

Even now that I am retired from teaching, I still enjoy ham radio, using my own station, and yet the greatest thrill of all is when someone asks me to show them what this thing called ham radio is all about. Once a teacher, always a teacher!

Chapter 24

Worst Case Scenario

Lest you, the reader, tire of my seeming to "blow my own horn," I am including some happenings that I feel will amply show that I, like all struggling high school teachers, also had my share of embarrassments and "come-uppances" during my early teaching years. I am only presenting those which taught me something. For example, after my layoff by that big aerospace company in Seattle, I soon obtained my secondary teaching credentials from the University of Washington. In order to increase my income while I searched for a permanent chemistry teaching position, for a full academic year I was doing substitute teaching in various high schools and junior high schools. This not only brought in a little income, but also provided me with a broad "bird's eye" view of that huge school district, and supplied me with considerable teaching experience, better preparing me for what lay ahead. One day I was hired to fill in for a junior high general science teacher who was out sick. Fortunately the teacher I was replacing had been on the subject of chemistry, my specialty, so I arrived feeling very confident about carrying on for her class. In order to get the students' attention, and meanwhile get across some major chemical principles, I decided to do my "signature" demonstration, which was the lab preparation of hydrogen gas, by displaying the dangerous "hydrogen blow-torch experiment." I was totally unconcerned about safety problems since I had no intention of allowing the young kids themselves (13- to 14-year-olds) to carry out the procedure, but would do it myself, as a demonstration. Hadn't I done this before, dozens of times, with no mishaps? I had pre-assembled the apparatus, consisting of a 250 ml Ehrlenmeyer Flask, connected with the usual one-hole rubber stopper, which had been fitted with a 3-inch piece of bent glass tubing, to allow a stream of the flammable gas to spew forth, once the reaction was initiated. I announced to the class, that morning, my intent, invited the group to gather around the front of the demonstration desk, so all could see the wondrous happening which would soon unfold, then said,

"Has anyone among you ever acted as a lab assistant for the teacher?" Immediately a rather scruffy, unkempt looking boy threw up his hand, so I commanded,

"Good, c'mon up here to help me with this!"

He was instantly at my side and we were ready to start the experiment. I added about 75 ml of previously diluted hydrochloric acid to the flask, then tossed in about 5 or 6 pieces of "mossy" zinc metal and replaced the rubber stopper and tubing set-up snugly. Immediately a small blast of gas issued out the end of the tubing, and I proclaimed,

"There comes our hydrogen gas. I know it just looks like steam, but I am about to show you that it is not."

At that point, I made the big boo-boo. I turned away, just for a second, leaving the apparatus bubbling and boiling and shooting out the flammable gas, as I had always done before, to grab a towel to wrap up the flask, as a safety measure. I turned back around just in time to see my little dork "lab assistant" pull his own cigarette lighter out of his pocket and **light the end of the delivery tube!** The tube, of course was still issuing both hydrogen gas, and air, so, horrified, I watched the flame travel quickly up inside the tube and back down into the generator flask where it loudly exploded, BLAM! I was stunned and temporarily deafened, and a bolt of fear went through me as I considered the possibilities. Had any flying broken glassware hit any of the students? I had not even required the closely watching class, or the little "assistant" to wear eye protection, since I had not planned to let them do the experiment! When the smoke cleared, I was afraid to look, but to my utter amazement—and I am not making this up—in utter defiance of the laws of physics, all of the shattered glassware plus all of the contents of the generator assembly had come straight back, hitting only me! It was running down my front, ruining my new sportcoat and dripping on to my nicely polished wingtips. Not one piece of that apparatus was ever found anywhere else in that room. It was as though a great unseen hand had placed itself between the exploding gadget and the kids. I was deliriously relieved, and did not stop shaking for some time. Except for my clothing, I was not harmed, but from that day forward, when I planned any experiments, I made it a point, always to ask myself, "What is the worst thing that could possibly happen? And how can I prevent that from happening?" I was not able to prevent **all** future mishaps with this approach, but I have to believe it helped mightily. As the next chapter will illustrate, I had much more yet to learn in this regard.

Chapter 25

Heed Your Own "Better Judgment"

A couple of weeks before I was to start as the new "chemistry prof," late one hot August afternoon in the chemistry lab-classroom which I would soon occupy, I met with the elderly silver-haired Jesuit priest whose position I would be taking, to see how he had done things and to request his "handy-dandy tips" on successful lab procedure as it had been carried out at the school. He was most cooperative and gave me full access to all his resources; then he began to show me where and how chemicals and apparatus had been stored and distributed to the students. Everything seemed reasonable until he showed me how the kids would obtain the chemicals themselves. He stored the students' chemicals in good sized trays of 4 or 5 rows of twenty or so: 1 ounce vials with their names on coded labels—on the **CAPS of the vials**! I, being a neophyte, and thinking to myself that he must know what had been working, unfortunately said nothing, even though my gut instinct told me this was all wrong.

In my chemistry program, the first two or three lab sessions did not call for chemicals, so all went well for a month or two, but soon I and a couple of my students would pay, big-time, for that poor judgment call. One fateful day in third-period (my third chem class of that day), my students were preparing oxygen gas by the thermal decomposition of potassium chlorate, a snow-white crystalline substance, and everything was apparently going well, as it had the previous two lab periods. The students were expressing the usual gasps of delight from watching the interesting properties of the gas as they carried out various tests on bottles of the gas they had captured by water displacement. I was roaming around the room checking the students procedures randomly, as was my custom, when a student near the back of the room raised his hand excitedly saying

"Mr. Kromholtz, we've got a problem. Please come help us!"

I went back to their lab station and noticed they were getting no oxygen from their apparatus, in contrast to t the other kids, and immediately I could see why. I said,

"Guys, the reason you're getting no oxygen is because you have forgotten to add the black manganese dioxide catalyst. Notice the contents of your generator tube are snow white. If the catalyst were present it would appear gray-black. Just add a little M-N-O-2. I'm sure it will work then!"

Then I hurried off to assist other groups with various difficulties. I was roughly 15 to 20 feet away from that group, facing away from them and engrossed in helping another lab group when BLAMMO! The biggest explosion I would ever encounter in school laboratory work just stunned the whole class. We were all temporarily deafened, and when the smoke cleared a little I glanced around to see everyone just **frozen** in place! Some had been pouring chemicals, others had been lighting Bunsen burners. Still others were about to introduce glowing wooden splints to a bottle of pure oxygen. But they were all stone statues now, deathly afraid that the very next step might cause their experiment to explode, too! They had all followed my major lab rule which was: **"When in doubt, stop and do nothing until you are sure what to do next."**

Then I saw the real bad news. There, fumbling around the back of the room, blood spurting from his cut upper arm was a boy from that original group I had just advised! Sending a boy running to inform the office, I raced to his side and, remembering my first aid training, tried to use the "pressure-points" to curb the bleeding—TO NO AVAIL!

This lad was a big football player type, and his upper arms were so well developed, the muscle obscured them. Next I ran to the storage room for our first-aid kit, retrieved a tourniquet, and was placing it when paramedics from the doctors' office up the street arrived and took over. They transported the hapless kid to their clinic, quickly "repaired" him and he was back in school that afternoon, none the worse for wear, and seeming to enjoy being the center of all this attention. (His lab partner, having sustained a small cut on his cheek, stayed away from my class for two days!) Classes were canceled for the remainder of that day, so I carefully inspected the "scene of the crime" alone, when I had the first opportunity. At first I couldn't imagine what had gone wrong since I had seen that experiment work successfully many times before. Then I spotted it! There, lying on the lab desk lay an opened vial of red phosphorus (a dangerously volatile substance) instead of the black catalyst powder I had directed those kids to add to the heated test tube of potassium chlorate. The **caps** of the two vials had been **SWITCHED** (probably unwittingly by students from the previous lab class). I knew right then and there that I should have listened to that little niggling voice in me that hot, August day, when I was first shown those chemical trays with **labels on the lids** by the previous chemistry teacher. Now it seemed clear why there were so many pock-marks and holes in the lab tables s in that class. That must have been a wild course at this school in past years! I immediately realized that I had to make some serious changes in lab procedure, and after carefully labeling all of the vials themselves, I even vowed, henceforth, never to pass out any chemicals to the students except those which were required for that particular experiment. I got a big lesson hammered home that day: always follow your **own** best judgment. It was only after many weeks of successful lab sessions that the rest of the school began to trust in the safety of my laboratories again.

Chapter 26

Rules are Rules

The previous chapters illustrate how much I had to learn regarding needed safety precautions when dealing with teenagers in the chemistry laboratory. In point of fact, I was to encounter other close calls, but because of my newly acquired wariness, followed by a much more intricately structured body of mandatory safety regulations that I speedily implemented, nothing even remotely approaching the incidents mentioned above ever happened again in my lab sessions.

One example of a near disaster, prevented by a fortunate regulation, comes immediately to mind: One afternoon, during the last class of the day, which happened to be a lab session, I was wandering around near the front of the class as the students were generally successfully carrying out what should have been a simple, innocuous experiment, when, right in front of me, a boy screamed as the test tube he was looking into popped with a juicy "fwoop" sound spewing the nasty contents into his face. I noticed immediately what had caused the unexpected result. "Tim," having successfully finished the assigned experiment, had gotten bored, and, breaking one of my cardinal rules (namely, "Always follow the Directions") had mixed together certain chemical substances "to see what would happen." As I handed him a baking soda solution-soaked towel with which to wipe his face, I told the class

"Thank goodness Tim was wearing his safety glasses, as you all are, or he would likely have been blinded. There is an old, obsolete rule that Tim was (unfortunately) also following: 'When All Else Fails, Read the Directions.' The rule should read 'ALWAYS Follow the Directions,' right?" The class broke into relieved laughter, as Tim wiped the chemicals off his face. Tim did get some minor facial burns, but no scarring, and I just got even more adamant about everyone learning safety rules

Another similar happening is forever etched in my memory: We were in the process of studying the acids and bases, as all general chemistry classes eventually must do. I had assigned the class a lab session involving the study of the most well-known properties of the three common strong mineral acids, namely hydrochloric, nitric, and sulfuric acids, respectively. The students were carrying out the experiments described in detail on their guide sheets, with considerable success, if the excited exclamations were any indication. I was looking around at the various partnerships, trying, as always, to nip in the bud any possible problems which might arise, when I noticed a girl who was getting frustrated because she couldn't get a certain dilution effect to happen as predicted in the instructions. I moved to her side and saw right away she had mistakenly reached for the sulfuric instead of the hydrochloric acid called for in the directions. It turns out that, unlike the benign result of mixing hydrochloric acid with water, mixing sulfuric acid with water can be decidedly dangerous, unless a specific procedure is scrupulously followed. All the previous week I had hammered home the ubiquitous lab rule, **"Do as you oughtta, add acid to watta,"** and she had, fortunately, remembered! Her resulting solution did heat up some, but did not pop, throwing about a dangerous acid-water mixture, as I have seen before, when water is carelessly added to concentrated sulfuric acid. I called the class's attention to her desk and said,

"Let me have your attention! Mona here just saved herself a serious mishap, because she remembered that little 'stupid' rule you guys made fun of last week during the pre-lab session: 'Do as you oughtta, add acid to watta.' Good work, Mona, I'll bet Ed, here is not ever going to be afraid to be your lab partner from now on! Everyone, be super-careful to choose the correct acid called for in each experiment, and 'Do as you oughtta, add acid to watta,' whenever dilutions are called for!"

Chapter 27

The Digital Revolution

I had been teaching electronics along with chemistry for some years and as I mentioned above (Chapter 23, "Hamming It Up") had emphasized the home entertainment and radio aspects of it because of my own training emphasis through my Bell & Howell Schools experience and, of course, my love of ham radio, much of which is, itself, electronics. This meant that my knowledge was mainly on the "linear" or "analog" area of the science and now, in the late 70's there was emerging a brand new, very exciting branch of electronics called digital, and I could plainly see that if I was to maintain my credibility as an instructor in modern electronics, I would soon need to get some serious training in this up-and-coming technology. Once again lady luck smiled on me: Bell & Howell Schools, through DeVry Institute, conferred upon me a fully paid correspondence course "fellowship" in modern "Digital Industrial Electronics" which I eagerly accepted and successfully completed. Later, I took an intensive two-week seminar at the University of Idaho in "Digital Integrated Circuit Design." I was now able to add a section of this technology to my electronics classes at the high school. Also, about this time, personal computers were becoming affordable (due to the appearance of the IBM format) and everyone began to ask us electronics types, "How do these amazing devices really work?" Therefore, once again I needed to learn more! I began to purchase various paperbacks on computer electronics, and spent many long summer hours reading up on this subject. I even eventually decided to build my own little working minicomputer in order to achieve the kind of "feel" for this subject I felt I needed to teach this subject confidently in this "brave new world" we all seemed destined to share. In order to accomplish this goal I had to teach myself about microprocessors and about machine-language programming, often spending considerable summer hours alone in my lab-classroom, reading and "breadboarding" the necessary circuitry to make my little creation finally work. And one day, it did! I was so thrilled when my little creation actually carried out the simple task I had programmed it to do, I just leaped up onto a lab table, shouting, "YES, YES!" (I don't think I was overheard by anyone at the time, although I would have proudly shown off the simple gadget to anyone interested , so high was I to see that all this stuff really worked.)

Next I decided it was time to spend some serious money and invest in my own personal computer, and promptly got hooked on this as well, even mastering that quirky, cryptic then-ubiquitous operating system called "DOS" in order to work my barely adequate first "p.c." I converted my teaching documentation, tests, problem sheets, etc. entirely to computer word processor format and found this wonderful to behold, but my next project, as we'll see in a later chapter, saved my "fanny," big-time, down the road a little. I had developed a case of severe "bursitis" (shoulder-centered arthritis) in my right shoulder because of the huge amount of chalkboard writing I routinely did, so I began to envision my classroom with a computer-based teaching station system employing a drawing program that would serve as my chalkless chalkboard, wherein I would be able to display everything I was seeing on my computer monitor on a big movie-type screen up and behind me, using one of the new computer projectors—and all this allowed me to face my class for interaction while doing so! I did my writing with a computer-connected digitizer "drawing pad" complete with a pen-like stylus or wand. This turned out to be a great idea, adding nifty, new, unforeseen powers to my bag of tricks almost daily. For example, erasures were now not only dustless, but were instantaneous. In addition, I could call up frames of equations, pictures of working apparatus, and even home-made animations, in multiple colors, to emphasize certain concepts; all of this was enhanced a thousand-fold with the advent of Microsoft's "Windows" operating system. Not only did all this technology make my classes a "hit" with the students, but it made teaching easier for me, both physically and intellectually. It was the late 80's and I was flyin' high, my classes full to overflowing with interested, excited students, but on November 9th, 1995, everything was to change drastically for me, as you'll see in the next chapter! Didn't Sinatra sing something like "Flyin' high in April, shot down in May"?

Chapter 28

Every Glass a Dribble Glass

I had just finished conferring with a string of parents concerning their students' recent progress in my class or classes that chilly fall early afternoon. Feeling very relaxed and sanguine about things, I drove home, intending to spend the remainder of my now free afternoon cleaning up my leaf-littered lawn, hopefully before it was buried as usual by the first snowfall of the year. My next-door neighbor, a sweet, friendly lady, was already hard at work in her own front yard, busily raking away. I left my car in my driveway, entered my home and started a pot of beef stew warming on the electric range. My wife, Sharon, was at work, as usual, at midday, and with all four of our children now on their own, I had the run of the place. I moseyed out to the garage, picked up some lawn and garden tools and implements and headed out to get to work on that front yard, totally covered with maple and horse-chestnut tree debris. The neighbor lady and I exchanged small talk for a few minutes, which required me to holler loudly to be heard over the roar of my little, portable, gasoline powered "Echo Shred n'Vac" Lawn Groomer. I was making considerable progress, making a number of trips to my back yard compost heap to dump load after load of shredded leaves, maple seeds and horse chestnuts ("buckeyes" as they are called in the Eastern United States) and was enjoying the superficial conversation with my neighbor, when **suddenly I found that I could not speak without biting my tongue!** Noticing that I was also feeling a bit weak, I figured that I must be hungry, since I had not yet had my lunch, so I excused myself and made my way back to my kitchen and that now-ready stew that my wife had prepared before she had left for work that morning. Although swallowing was strangely, now, not easy, I downed a small bowl of the delicious dish, but noticed little improvement in my energy level. I knew, now, that something was wrong, and decided to head upstairs for a little bedrest. It was not easy to get up those stairs, but I managed it and thought to myself, "Maybe you had better call Sharon to tell her you are 'coming down with something' and would be napping a little." But when I reached for the phone, it **felt like five or six ten-pound lead weights had been strapped to my left arm!** Now picking up the receiver with my unaffected right arm, I was able to contact my wife with a now more shocking message. Having worked in the area of medical law for many years, she recognized the symptoms, and, telling me to stay right where I was, namely in our bedroom, she informed her boss of the emergency and drove the four or five miles quickly home to be at my side. One look at my condition and she immediately phoned 911 and requested an ambulance, to get me to the ER pronto. Paramedics arrived with dispatch and I was soon undergoing multiple tests. The tests showed that I had suffered a massive cerebral hemorrhage (which the doctors called a "bleed") and a few minutes later, suffered a second "re-bleed," which, my gathering relatives and friends were told, had me "at death's door." All the doctors later explained to us that this "leak" happened because of a congenital weak spot in a major blood vessel in my brain, and would most likely have been inevitable. (My favorite aunt on my father's side had died of the same thing years before.) All through this ordeal, I myself had no idea of the peril of my condition, as I had been essentially unconscious, oddly dreaming cartoon-style dreams, which, I'm now given to understand, had told the neurologists of the urgent nature of my condition! (I never did see any tunnel with a bright light at the end, with the fabled warm, welcoming feelings, or any of that; I only watched "Snagglepuss," the Hanna-Barbera cartoon cat, chase the "miserable meeces" around in my head, saying "heavens to murgatroyd" as legions of neurosurgeons, neurologists and cardio-pulmonary specialists (I had sustained a collapsed lung at this point), some of whom had been my students in previous years, hovered around me, running CAT scans, x-rays, and ultrasounds, as they came to the scary conclusion that I would need brain surgery if I were to survive! Fortunately (although I suspect luck had little to do with it, what with the torrent of prayers issued by my family and friends, I'm told), a highly regarded, expert neurosurgeon just happened to be on duty.

Although he was not overly optimistic about my chances, he gave in to mounting pressure from my loved ones, and eventually operated and saved my life, although he could not alleviate the hemiplegia (left-side paralysis), which I still suffer from today. (This book was typed with one hand.) Through the expert, daily application of a newly invented device called the "IPIPPB" (Intermittent Placement Intermittent Positive Pressure Breathing) apparatus, the pulmonary doctors and technicians brought my collapsed lung back to normal. As it turned out, my verbal capacities and, amazingly my long-term memory were unaffected, so, it was theoretically likely I could continue to teach, although I could no longer spit, whistle, or carry a tune, all abilities I am still without as I write this book! I did suffer a few annoying,odd effects. For one thing, I incurred a tendency to **drool** whenever I concentrated strongly—I had to work hard to overcome that one, since I was sure that would not "go over" with high school kids. Secondly, even the slightest hint of poignancy, including any small surge of patriotism, school spirit, or even romance, would provoke me to break down and blubber like a child. Thus, I was forced not to "go there," as they say nowadays, very often in class. In addition to these symptoms, I was, for some weeks, unable to drink fluids from an ordinary tumbler without dribbling water down the left side of my face. I had first experienced this particular symptom while still in the hospital, and at first I actually thought the nurses were playing practical jokes on me by slipping me dribble-glasses! My poor family must have found that time especially trying.

Chapter 29

Technology to the Rescue

Although I still carry some of these burdens, I have not been seriously hampered by them, either now or then. However, another even bigger challenge to my return to teaching still lay ahead for me. As I finished up first my month's stay in the hospital followed by another month in a nursing home, I was absolutely swamped by a continuous strings of visitors, including family, friends, and students (both current and past). I can see now it was that outflow of love, support and prayers—to me, very surprising—that convinced me to go back and give it another try. I think the nurses were actually rather relieved to see my departure because of the huge number of visitors I had brought into that sparkling clean little nursing home. However, I reasoned:

"How would I be able to run my classes without the use of my left arm and leg?"

Then it hit me: "Maybe I could do it anyway, because of that computer-based lecturing system I had put together!" After all, I had been successfully running my classes,not labs from a sitting position for months, hadn't I? So back I went the next fall, teaching part-time, but finding I could still "cut the mustard" only with the help of an adult assistant for running laboratory sessions. The school even specially hired a very well-trained, most cooperative young biochemist, not only to assist me with my classes, but to teach a few classes of lower level chemistry on his own. I soon discovered that in order to make things work properly, in my "own" classes, I had to remain personally in charge of **G**rading, **O**rganization and **D**iscipline. (Notice the initials "**G.O.D.**": With the tremendous deference and respect paid to me by everyone, you would have sworn there was a connection!) I think any successful teacher will find that he or she must be fully in charge of all three of those areas, at all times.

Just after my nursing home stint, I had undergone a few weeks of physical, occupational and speech therapy at a local rehab institute, and had regained some muscle use in that left leg: enough, fortunately, to allow me to stand for a short while and to make transfers from chair to chair and from and to automobile and toilet seats, all of which still contribute greatly to my level of comfort and enjoyment. But it was the incredibly fortunate development of that computer-based teaching station which, in the final analysis, made it possible for a person with my handicaps to continue teaching as I, in fact, did, for seven more years. When the students from my classes were asked by various administrators what Mr. Kromholtz was like since the "stroke," I learned they had invariably replied something like, "Oh, Mr. Kromholtz hasn't really changed at all, he just sits down a lot more than he used to!" I'm so glad I put in those last seven years. I met so many wonderful, new, young faces, made some great new friends, kept my mind active and enthusiastic, and even "salted away" a little more wherewithal for my upcoming retirement.

Chapter 30

Seeds Can Take Root,
Even When You Least Expect It

My wife and I were attending a wedding in the early 90's of one of our young teachers, who, years before, had also been my student. As we waited to be escorted to our seat in the church, I noticed that most of the wedding party were also previous students of mine. In fact the very usher who smartly stepped up to guide us to our designated pew and asked us "Are you friends of the bride, or friends of the groom?" I immediately recognized as Mark Gormly, a boy who had been a rather unenthusiastic but talented student of mine many years back, and a classmate of the groom. As we sauntered together down the aisle of the huge, Romanesque style old church toward our appointed seats, Mark suddenly turned and said to me,

"Mr. Kromholtz, it's nice to see you again. Guess what I do for a living nowadays." When I assured him I had no idea, he said, with a big smile,

"Believe it or not, I'm a chemist. I work for _____"

(he named a well-known local mining/manufacturing firm). I was truly amazed, since this particular youth, although a fine football running back, and a bright science student, had not previously shown that much overt interest in **my** subject. I replied,

"Wow, that's great, Mark! I had no idea you would go that route."

I have, over the years, had quite a few other, similar pleasant surprises in this regard, and I have come to believe that high school students very often may not show **immediate** growth, either intellectually or emotionally, but they are taking it all in, and some time down the road, seeds of interest that you planted during these **super-formative** years will take root and blossom.

Teachers need not lose heart if their charges don't always respond immediately. If you, the teacher, were a "class act," they'll remember you fondly in later years, and profit in ways you can't even imagine. What an important profession! Be the best you can be at it, both in your subject matter and in your demeanor. You are a major role model: next to their parents, maybe the most important they will ever have. That's both a privilege and a scary responsibility, isn't it? I loved it, although it kept me "on the edge of red" for many years. It was not as glamorous as working on the AEC's "Pluto" program or NASA's

Saturnrn-5", or "Dyna-Soar" projects, as I had done before taking up teaching. Nevertheless, I am proudest of those teaching years because I feel I was making my greatest contribution to our society then. I think I was built to be there in front of a high school classroom, to be 37 years "on the edge of red."

About the Author

My name is **Kurt L. Kromholtz.** I was born on March 4th, 1937 in Libby, Montana to immigrant parents Louis F. Kromholtz and Winifred M. Stevens.

We moved to Spokane, Washington in 1940 where I grew up. (Spokane I consider my home town.)

I attended St. Aloysius Grade School from 1944 until 1951. I then attended Gonzaga High School, (later called Gonzaga Prep) and graduated in 1955.

I enrolled as a chemistry major at Gonzaga University in the fall of 1955 and graduated from that institution with a Bachelor of Science degree in chemistry in the spring of 1959. The title of my undergraduate thesis was "Mathematical Aspects of Solid Rocket Propellant Chemistry".

On May 30th of that spring I married my sweetheart, Sharon Crawford We drove to California (this drive originally conceived to be a honeymoon trip as well as getting me to my place of employment)where I took a job as a high temperature chemist with the Lawrence Livermore National Laboratory or LLNL, (then called The University of California Radiation Laboratory).

Until the fall of 1961 I worked on the Atomic Energy Commission's Project Pluto (nuclear ramjet) in the area of high temperature materials research.

I then took a job with The Boeing Company in Seattle, Washington where I did similar high temperature materials research for NASA's Project Dyna-Soar (the original space shuttle design).

When that project was canceled in 1963 due to redundancy I then did cryogenic materials research and development on NASA's Saturn-5 booster program (Apollo Moonshot booster rocket) until I was laid off along with a thousand other "engineers" in 1963.

I next decided to enter the field of teaching and spent a year at the University of Washington in Seattle and obtained my certification as a secondary school teacher

I then landed a short-term job as mathematics professor at Highline Community College in Burien, Washington,and then, when that job ran out, I did secondary school substitute teaching in many high schools and junior high schools in the Seattle area for about a year(1964-5) until I finally landed my career position as chemistry instructor at my old Alma Mater, Gonzaga Preparatory School back in my home town, Spokane, Washington, in 1965.

I received a National Science Foundation Fellowship to Purdue University in 1966 and spent four summers at that school, in West Lafayette, Indiana , from 1967 to 1970 , procuring an M.S. in chemistry in 1970.

I taught at Gonzaga Prep in the fields of chemistry, electronics, ham radio and computers until 1995 when a serious "stroke" (actually a cerebral hemorrhage), knocked me temporarily out of action. I nearly died but brain surgery saved my life, but left me hemiplegic. After some rehab and after an assistant was hired to help me with lab work, I returned to part-time teaching duties even though my left side including my left arm and leg were paralyzed, and still are.

After seven more years of teaching in this way I finally retired in 2002, and have been writing ever since. My wife of 46 years, Sharon, and I have four children, Tim, Karen, Kevin and Bryan, all on their own now. We have eleven grandchildren and two great grandchildren.

I am enjoying retirement very much due to lots of loving family and friends and my many hobbies including ham radio, computers , German cars and, of course, writing!

Made in United States
North Haven, CT
22 July 2023

39333742R00093